Copycat C~

The best beginner's guide over 150 re   asty dishes

from famous restaurants fo   ag home

JAMES LEWIS

Table of Contents

INTRODUCTION

Preparing and cooking food at home is now easy and now you can taste your favorite dishes at home cooking. You will find proven recipes from your favorite fastfood restaurant Cracker Barrel, Subway, Taco Bell, and Burger King in this volume. With these recipes, you will have the same final flavor by saving money and having fun. All the recipes here are easy to follow and the ingredients are not hard to find! Say goodbye to many hours. wait in a restaurant to have a table. Say goodbye to long lines just to buy food on tour and say goodbye to spending more than you should be eating out. Cooking at home can be time consuming and create a mess you need to clean up, but once you prepare a particular dish and eat it, you will be proud and amazed to have made a popular snack - a delicious meal with your own hands. . Here are some good reasons why you should start cooking at home and how you can cook at home. Cost It is much cheaper to buy your ingredients at the local farmers market. Sometimes you can even harvest it in your garden. Cooking at home will eliminate the cost of labor, restaurant maintenance, additional taxes and gasoline. There are many avenues where you can cut costs by cooking at home compared to food. Health This is best for making imitation homemade recipes. The recipes give an accurate measurement of the ingredients, but you can modify some of them depending on how you prefer the flavor. Whether you want to minimize spice or add more to your food is up to you. You can get rid of ingredients you are allergic to, or use ingredients with a lower sugar or fat content. The possibilities are endless. You have full control over that. Quality All the recipes you will find here have been tested. I have checked repeatedly to make sure you have the correct ingredients and the correct steps to make your favorite dish. Of course, you can go online to find recipes that claim to be copies of popular restaurants. Yes, its free. And that is why it is free. These are not real recipes for imitation purposes. It's not even close. I've tried a couple, and to be honest, they weren't close, they weren't even good. I will show you how to get the real imitation recipes and regain your freedom. One of the biggest challenges in eating at home is getting it running on budget, but it's much cheaper than eating out. However, the cost of food increases each year, with careful planning and exploration of new options. There are many ways to enjoy the most popular recipes at home on a budget. Often prices vary from one store or market to another and quality selection while maintaining the cost of charging your supermarket can be challenging. Consider the following options when preparing for your following trip to the supermarket: Explore and visit local farmers markets. Some local markets may specialize in certain species, while others are widespread and have many local farmers, artisans, and products. In some cases, buying in the future may offer the opportunity for discounts on certain products

BREAKFAST AND BRUNCH RECIPES

1. French Toast

Preparation Time: 10 minutes Cooking time: 25 minutes Servings: 8

Ingredients:

8 slices Texas toast or sourdough bread 4 eggs 1 cup milk 2 tablespoons sugar 4 teaspoons vanilla extract 2 pinches salt Butter and syrup for serving

Directions: Whisk the eggs, milk, sugar, vanilla, and salt together in a large bowl. Heat a griddle or skillet over medium heat. Spray with nonstick cooking spray. Dip each slice of bread in egg mixture, letting it soak for 25–30 seconds on each side. Transfer the slices to the griddle or skillet and cook for 2–3 minutes on each side, or until golden brown. Serve with butter and syrup. Nutrition: Calories 235 Protein 25 Carbs 16 Fat 5

2. Buttermilk Biscuits

Preparation Time: 15 minutes Cooking Time: 15 minutes Servings: 10

Ingredients:

2 cups all-purpose flour 2 teaspoons baking powder 1/2 teaspoon baking soda 1/2 teaspoon salt 1/4 cup shortening 3/4 cup buttermilk

Directions Preheat oven to 450°. In a bowl, combine flour, baking powder, baking soda and salt; cut in shortening until the mixture resembles coarse crumbs. Stir in buttermilk; knead dough gently. Roll out to 1/2-in. thickness. Cut with a 2-1/2-in. biscuit cutter and place on a lightly greased baking sheet. Bake until golden brown, 10-15 minutes. Freeze option: Freeze cooled biscuits in a resealable freezer container. To use, heat in a preheated 350° oven 15-20 minutes. Nutrition: Calories: 142, Fat: 5g, Cholesterol: 1mg, Sodium: 281mg, Carbohydrate: 20g, Protein: 3g

3. McMuffin Sandwich

Preparation Time 10 minutes Cooking Time 20 minutes Serving: 5

Ingredients:

6 English muffins Eight spoonfuls of salted butter 12 slices American cheese 12 large eggs Six slices Canadian bacon

Directions

The oven should be preheated to the temperature of 300 ° F. Fry the eggs until they are fried well, using a round egg mold just to want a round egg. Warm the Canadian sliced bacon by frying it on the griddle, too. Slice in half the English muffins, then toast them in a toaster. Place a thin layer of butter on each half of the English toasted muffin. In every English muffin, add a slice of cheese to the bottom half. Place the English muffins on a sheet of cookies and into the oven, allowing the cheese to melt slightly; it will take only about 3 to 5 minutes. Remove from the oven the English muffins, and start layering. You must add an egg to the sandwich's coated bottom, add another layer of cheese onto the egg, add a second egg, then a slice of Canadian bacon, followed by the top of the English muffin. Serve warm, and enjoy! Nutrition: Calories: 558, Total Fat: 36g, Saturated Fat: 18g, Trans Fat: 1g, Unsaturated Fat: 14g, Cholesterol: 453mg,

4. The Spinach and Artichoke Dip

Preparation Time: 5 minutes Cooking Time: 30 minutes Servings: 10

Ingredients:

10-ounce bag spinach, diced 14-ounce cans artichoke hearts, diced 1 cup Parmesan-Romano cheese mix, grated 2 cups mozzarella cheese, grated 16 ounces' garlic alfredo sauce 8 ounces' cream cheese, softened

Directions Combine all ingredients in a bowl. Mix well. Transfer into a slow cooker. Set on high and cook for 30 minutes. Serve while hot. Nutrition: Calories: 228 Fat: 15 g Carbs: 12 g Protein: 13 g Sodium: 418 mg

5. Pork Sage Sausage

Preparation Time: 5 minutes Cooking Time: 20 minutes Servings: 4

Ingredients:

1-pound ground pork 1 teaspoon salt 1/2teaspoon dried parsley
1/4teaspoon rubbed sage 1/4teaspoon black pepper, ground 1/4teaspoon
dried thyme 1/4teaspoon coriander 1/4teaspoon seasoned salt

Directions

Mix all ingredients in a bowl. Shape into patties. Then, cook in a pan on
medium heat until meat is brown on both sides and cooked. Serve.
Nutrition: Calories: 313 Fat: 24 g Carbs: 4 g Protein: 19 g Sodium: 646 mg

6. The Spinach and Artichoke Dip from Applebee's

Preparation Time: 5 minutes Cooking Time: 30 minutes Servings: 10

Ingredients:

10-ounce bag spinach, diced 14-ounce cans artichoke hearts, diced 1 cup
Parmesan-Romano cheese mix, grated 2 cups mozzarella cheese, grated 16
ounces' garlic alfredo sauce 8 ounces' cream cheese, softened

Directions

Combine all ingredients in a bowl. Mix well. Transfer into a slow cooker. Set
on high and cook for 30 minutes. Serve while hot. Nutrition: Calories: 228
Fat: 15 g Carbs: 12 g Protein: 13 g Sodium: 418 mg

7. McDonald's Sausage Egg McMuffin

Preparation Time: 10 minutes Cooking Time: 15 minutes Servings: 4

Ingredients:

4 English muffins, cut in half horizontally 4 slices American processed cheese 1/2tablespoon oil 1-pound ground pork, minced 1/2teaspoon dried sage, ground 1/2teaspoon dried thyme 1 teaspoon onion powder 3/4 teaspoon black pepper 3/4 teaspoon salt 1/2teaspoon white sugar 4 large 1/3 -inch onion ring slices 4 large eggs 2 tablespoons water

Directions

Preheat oven to 300°F. Cover one half of muffin with cheese, leaving one half uncovered. Transfer both halves to a baking tray. Place in oven. For the sausage patties, use your hands to mix pork, sage, thyme, onion powder, pepper, salt, and sugar in a bowl. Form into 4 patties. Make sure they are slightly larger than the muffins. Heat oil in a pan. Cook patties on both sides for at least 2 minutes each or until all sides turn brown. Remove tray of muffins from oven. Place cooked sausage patties on top of the cheese on muffins. Return tray to the oven. In the same pan, position onion rings flat into a single layer. Crack one egg inside each of the onion rings to make them round. Add water carefully into the sides of the pan and cover. Cook for 2 minutes. Remove tray of muffins from the oven. Add eggs on top of patties, then top with the other muffin half. Serve warm. Nutrition: Calories:453 Fat: 15 g Carbs: 67 g Protein: 15 g Sodium: 1008 mg

8. Ihop's Buttermilk Pancake

Preparation time: 5 minutes Cooking time: 8 minutes Servings: 8 to 10

Ingredients

11/4cups of all-purpose flour 1 teaspoon of baking soda 1 teaspoon of baking powder 11/4cups of granulated sugar 1 pinch salt 1 egg 11/4cups of buttermilk 1/4cup cooking oil

Directions

Preheat your pan by leaving it over medium heat while you're preparing the batter. Take all of your dry ingredients and blend them. Take all of your wet ingredients and blend them. Carefully combine the dry mixture into the wet mixture until everything is mixed together entirely. Melt some butter in your pan. Slowly pour batter into the pan until you've got a 5-inch circle. Flip the pancake when its edges seem to possess hardened. Cook the opposite side of the hotcake also. Repeat steps six through eight until your batter is finished. Serve with softened butter and syrup. Nutrition: Calories 180.1, Total Fat 7.9g, Carbohydrates 23.2g Protein 4.1 g, Sodium 271.6mg

9. Waffle House's Waffle

Preparation Time: 5 minutes Cooking Time: 20 minutes Servings: 6

Ingredients 11/2cups of all-purpose flour 1 teaspoon of salt 1/2teaspoon of baking soda 1 egg 1/2cup + 1 tablespoon of granulated white sugar 2 tablespoons of butter, softened 2 tablespoons of shortening 1/2cup of half-and-half 1/2cup of milk 1/4cup of buttermilk 1/4teaspoon of vanilla

Directions Prepare the dry mixture by sifting the flour into a bowl and mixing it with soda's salt and bicarbonate. In a medium bowl, lightly beat an egg when the egg has become frothy, hammer in the butter, sugar, and shortening. When the mixture is thoroughly mixed, hammer in the half-and-half, vanilla, milk, and buttermilk, continue beating the mixture until it's smooth. While beating the wet mixture, slowly pour in the dry mix to combine thoroughly and take away all the lumps. Chill the batter overnight (optional but recommended; if you can't chill the mixture overnight, leave it for 15 to twenty minutes). Take the batter out of the refrigerator. Preheat and grease your waffle iron. Cook each waffle for 3 to four minutes. Serve with butter and syrup. Nutrition: Calories 313.8, Total Fat 12.4g, Carbohydrates 45g, Protein 5.9g Sodium 567.9mg

10. Breakfast Muffins

Preparation time: 20 minutes Cooking time: 20 minutes Servings: 2

Ingredients:

New Thyme 1.49fl oz   Almond milk Handfuls lettuce cooked veggies Salt Pepper 1 tbsp. coriander 3oz granola

Directions

Preheat the oven to 375 degrees. Coat 6 cups of a muffin tin with cooking spray or line with paper liners. Crack the eggs into an outsized bowl. Use a Braun MultiQuick Hand Blender or a whisk to blend the eggs until smooth; this may take but a moment. Add the spinach, bacon, and cheese to the egg mixture and stir to mix. Divide the egg mixture evenly among the muffin cups. Bake for 15-18 minutes or until eggs are set. Serve immediately or store in the refrigerator until able to eat. Top with diced tomatoes and parsley if desired. Nutrition: Calories 440 Fat: 28g Carbohydrates: 28g Protein:19g

11. Loaded Hash Brown Casserole

Preparation Time: 10 minutes Cooking time: 20 minutes Servings: 4

Ingredients: 1 pound sausage 3 tablespoons chopped red bell pepper 1/2cup grated American cheese 1/2cup grated sharp cheddar cheese 1/2cup grated Monterey Jack cheese 11/2cups grated Colby cheese (divided) 2 tablespoons butter 2 tablespoons flour 2 cups milk 2 pounds frozen hash browns

Directions: Preheat the oven to 350degree F. Cook the sausage in a large skillet over medium-high heat while breaking it into bite-sized pieces. Add the red pepper and cook. Drain any grease and set aside. Melt 2 tablespoons of butter in another skillet. Stir in the flour and let it cook for a minute or so until it starts to brown. Whisk in 1/4cup of the milk and continue to cook and stir until the mixture thickens. Then whisk in the remaining milk and cook a bit longer. It will thicken up again; when it does, add the cheeses, reserving 1 cup of the Colby cheese for the casserole's top. In a bowl, combine the hash browns, the cheese sauce you just prepared, and the cooked sausage. Mix so that everything is combined, then pour into a baking dish and top with the reserved Colby cheese. Cook for about 45 minutes or until the cheese is melted and the casserole is bubbly. Nutrition: Calories 135 Protein 25 Carbs 16 Fat 5

12. Blueberry Syrup

Preparation Time: 10 minutes Cooking time: 30 minutes Servings: 3

Ingredients: 2 cups blueberries 1/2cup sugar 1 cup water 1 tablespoon cornstarch

Directions

Combine the cornstarch with 2 tablespoons of water in a small bowl. Whisk until no longer clumpy and set aside. Combine the water, blueberries, and sugar in a saucepan. Bring the mixture to a boil, then reduce the heat and simmer for about 10 minutes or until it has reduced a bit. Stir in the cornstarch and whisk until well combined. Continue to simmer and stir until the sauce has thickened. When it has reached a syrup-like consistency, remove from heat. You can mix with an immersion blender if you choose. Serve with pancakes or waffles. Nutrition: Calories 215 Protein 25 Carbs 16 Fat 5 Egg

---

13. Spinach and Cheese Egg Soufflé

Preparation Time: 15 minutes Cooking Time: 25 minutes Servings: 4

Ingredients: 1 tube butter flake crescent rolls 6 eggs, divided 3 tablespoons milk 2 tablespoons heavy cream 1/4cup cheddar cheese, grated 1/4cup jack cheese, grated 1 tablespoon Parmesan cheese 3 tablespoons fresh spinach, mince 4 slices of bacon, cooked and crumbled Cooking spray 1/4teaspoon salt 1/4cup Asiago cheese, grated, divided

Directions Preheat oven to 375°F. Add 5 eggs, milk, heavy cream, cheddar cheese, jack cheese, parmesan cheese, spinach, bacon, and salt to a nonreactive bowl. Mix well until combined then heat in microwave for about 30 seconds. Stir, then microwave for another 20 seconds. Repeat about 5 times or until egg mixture is a bit thicker but still runny and uncooked. Roll out crescent roll dough. Make 4 rectangles by pressing together the triangles. Using a roll pin, stretch them out until they are 6in x 6in square. Coat ramekin with cooking spray and place flattened roll inside, making sure the edges are outside the ramekin. Add 1/3 cup egg mixture and then about 1/8 cup Asiago cheese. Wrap edges of the roll-on top. Repeat for remaining rolls. Whisk remaining egg with salt lightly in a bowl then, with a pastry brush, brush on top of each crescent roll dough. Place ramekins in the oven and bake for 20 minutes or until brown. Serve. Nutrition: Calories: 303 Fat: 25 g Saturated Fat: 11 g Carbs: 4 g Sugar: 1 g Fibers: 0 g Protein: 20 g Sodium: 749 mg

9

14. French Toasts

Preparation Time: 10 minutes Cooking Time: 12 minutes Servings: 6

Ingredients:

Batter 4 eggs 2/3 cup whole milk 1/3 cup flour 1/3 cup sugar 1/2teaspoon vanilla extract 1/4teaspoon salt 1/8 teaspoon cinnamon Other ingredients 6 slices bread loaf, sliced thick 3 tablespoons butter Powdered sugar for dusting Syrup as desired

Directions

Mix in the ingredients for batter in a bowl. Soak bread slices in batter one at a time for at least 30 seconds on both sides. Allow excess batter to drip off. Melt 1 tablespoon of butter in a pan, cook battered bread over medium heat for 2 minutes or until each side is golden brown. Move slice to a plate. Repeat with the remaining slices of bread, adding more butter to the pan if needed. Dust with powdered sugar, if desired, and with syrup poured on top. Nutrition: Calories: 264 Fat: 11 g Carbs: 33g Protein: 8g Sodium: 360 mg

15. Sonic's Super SONIC Copycat Burrito

Preparation Time: 10 minutes Cooking Time: 25 minutes Servings: 8

Ingredients: 50 tater tots, frozen 1-pound breakfast sausage patties 8 large eggs, beaten 2 tablespoons half and half Salt and pepper, to taste 1 tablespoon butter 6-inch flour tortillas 11/2cups cheddar cheese, grated .1 medium onion, diced 1/2cup pickled jalapeño peppers, sliced 3 roma tomatoes, sliced Salsa

Directions Cook tater tots per instructions on the package but cook them so they are a bit crispy. Set aside. In a pan, cook sausage patties. Break apart into large clumps until brown. Add eggs, half and half, salt, and pepper in a bowl. Whisk until well mixed. Heat butter in a pan over medium heat. Pour egg mixture and stir every now and then until scrambled. Remove from heat. Microwave tortillas until warm but still soft. Then, in a vertical line in the center, add cheddar cheese, eggs, cooked sausage, tater tots, onions, jalapeños, and tomato. Fold the ingredients using the outer flaps of the tortilla. Repeat with remaining ingredients and tortillas. Serve warm with salsa.   Nutrition: Calories: 636 Fat: 40 g Saturated Fat: 16 g Carbs: 39 g Sugar: 4 g Fibers: 3 g Protein: 28 g Sodium: 1381 mg

16. The French Toasts from Denny's

Preparation Time: 10 minutes Cooking Time: 12 minutes Servings: 6

Ingredients: Batter 4 eggs 2/3 cup whole milk 1/3 cup flour 1/3 cup sugar 1/2teaspoon vanilla extract 1/4teaspoon salt 1/8 teaspoon cinnamon Other ingredients 6 slices bread loaf, sliced thick 3 tablespoons butter Powdered sugar for dusting Syrup as desired

Directions: Mix in the ingredients for batter in a bowl. Soak bread slices in batter one at a time for at least 30 seconds on both sides. Allow excess batter to drip off. Melt 1 tablespoon of butter in a pan, cook battered bread over medium heat for 2 minutes or until each side is golden brown. Move slice to a plate. Repeat with the remaining slices of bread, adding more butter to the pan if needed. Dust with powdered sugar, if desired, and with syrup poured on top. Nutrition: Calories:

17. Jimmy Dean's Homemade Pork Sage Sausage

Preparation Time: 5 minutes Cooking Time: 20 minutes Servings: 4

Ingredients:

1-pound ground pork 1 teaspoon salt 1/2teaspoon dried parsley 1/4teaspoon rubbed sage 1/4teaspoon black pepper, ground 1/4teaspoon dried thyme 1/4teaspoon coriander 1/4teaspoon seasoned salt

Directions

Mix all ingredients in a bowl. Shape into patties. Then, cook in a pan on medium heat until meat is brown on both sides and cooked through. Serve. Nutrition: Calories: 313 Fat: 24 g Carbs: 4 g Protein: 19 g Sodium: 646 mg

18. Ihop's Scrambled Egg

Preparation Time: 5 minutes Cooking Time: 5 minutes Servings: 1

Ingredients 1/4cup pancake mix 1–2 tablespoons of o butter 6 large eggs Salt and pepper, to taste

Directions

Thoroughly beat the pancake mix and, therefore, the eggs together until no lumps or clumps remain. Butter a pan over medium heat. When the pan is hot enough, pour the egg mixture in the middle of the pan. Add the salt and pepper and let the mixture sit for a few minutes. When the egg starts cooking, start pushing the sides of the mixture toward the center of the pan. Continue until the whole mixture is cooked. Serve and luxuriate in. Nutrition: Calories 870, Total Fat 54g, Carbohydrates 9g, Protein 69g, Sodium 34.9 mg

19. Alice Springs Chicken from Outback

Preparation Time: 5 minutes Cooking Time: 2 hours 30 minutes Servings: 4

Ingredients Sauce: 1/2cup Dijon mustard 1/2cup honey 1/4cup mayonnaise 1 teaspoon fresh lemon juice Chicken Preparation: 4 chicken breast, boneless and skinless 2 tablespoons of butter 1 tablespoon olive oil 8 ounces fresh mushrooms, sliced 4 slices bacon, cooked and cut into 2-inch pieces 2 1/2cups of Monterrey Jack cheese, shredded Parsley for serving (optional)

Directions Preheat oven to 400 °F. Mix ingredients for the sauce in a bowl. Put the chicken in a Ziploc bag, and then add the sauce into the bag until only 1/4cup is left. Keep the remaining sauce in a container, cover, and refrigerate. Confirm to seal Ziploc bag tightly and gently shake until chicken is coated with sauce confine refrigerator for a minimum of 2 hours. Melt butter in a pan over medium heat. Add mushrooms and cook for five minutes or until brown. Remove from pan and place on a plate. Heat oil in an oven-safe pan. Place marinated chicken flat in the pan and cook for five minutes on all sides or until each side turns golden brown. Top with even amounts of mushroom, bacon, and cheese. Cover pan with an oven-safe lid then bakes for 10 to fifteen minutes until chicken is cooked through. Remove lid and bake a further 1-3 minutes until the cheese is all melted. Transfer onto a plate. Serve with remaining sauce on the side. Sprinkle chicken with parsley if desired Nutrition: Calories 888 Total Fat 56g Carbohydrates 41g Protein 59g Sodium 1043mg

APPETIZERS AND DRINKS

20. Mini Crab Cakes

Preparation time: 10 minutes Cooking time 4 minutes Servings: 4

Ingredients:

2 tablespoons mayonnaise 2 tablespoons green onion, minced (green part only) 2 tablespoons red bell pepper, minced 1/2beaten egg 1 teaspoon fresh parsley, minced 1 teaspoon Old Bay seasoning 1/2teaspoon prepared yellow mustard 1/2pound lump crab meat 3 tablespoons plain breadcrumbs 1/4cup panko breadcrumbs vegetable oil Remoulade Sauce: 1/2cup mayonnaise 2 teaspoons capers 2 teaspoons dill pickle slices, chopped 1 teaspoon lemon juice 1/2teaspoon fresh parsley, minced 1/2teaspoon paprika 1/2teaspoon chili powder 1/4teaspoon cayenne pepper 1/4teaspoon ground cumin 1/8 teaspoon salt

Directions

In a large bowl, combine the mayo, green onions, red pepper, egg, parsley, Old Bay, mustard, crab meat, and the plain bread crumbs. Gently mix the ingredients together. Don't over mix or the crab meat will fall apart too much. Working carefully, form the mixture into 4 equal-sized flat patties. Cover the patties with parchment paper and refrigerate for a couple of hours. Refrigerating will help the patty to set. In the meantime, mix all of the Remoulade sauce ingredients together, making sure it is well combined. After the crab cakes have had a chance to chill, heat enough oil in a large skillet so that the crab cake has enough to sit in. Pour the panko breadcrumbs in a shallow dish and dip each crab cake into the panko, then place it in the skillet and cook for 2 to 3 minutes on each side. Remove the crab cakes from the skillet and allow them to drain on a paper towel. Serve with the remoulade sauce. Nutrition: Calories: 289 Fat: 8.7 g Carbs: 25. 2 g Protein: 33.9 g Sodium: 331 mg

21. Cracker Barrel's Biscuits

Preparation Time: 15 minutes Cooking Time: 8 minutes Servings: 8

Ingredients:

2 cups self-rising flour 1/3 cup shortening 2/3 cup buttermilk Melted butter, to brush

Directions

Preheat oven to 450 °F. In a bowl, mix flour and shortening until mixture is loose and crumbly. Pour in buttermilk. Mix well. Sprinkle flour onto a smooth surface and flatten dough on top. Cut dough into desired shapes using biscuit cutters. Arrange onto a baking sheet. Place in oven and cook for 8 minutes. Apply melted butter on top using a brush. Serve. Nutrition: Calories: 194 Fat: 9 g Carbs: 24 g Protein: 4 g Sodium: 418 mg

22. Veggie-in-a-Blanket

Preparation Time: 10 minutes Cooking Time: 15 minutes Servings: 8

Ingredients:

4 slices of square cheese (cut diagonally to form triangles) 1 pack of veggie cocktail sausages   1 can of crescent roll dough   1 tbsp. of garlic and herb mix hot sauce (optional for dip)

Directions:

Preheat your oven to 350°F. Cut your dough into triangular shapes (along the perforated lines). Place a slice of triangular cheese and a mini sausage along the widths end of each pastry triangle. Add a drop of garlic and herb mix into each triangle pastry, then roll the pastries around the mini sausages, tucking the leftover pastry at the bottom of each roll. Place the rolls on a baking tray and bake for 14 minutes. Serve while hot. Nutrition: Calories 123 Carbs 3.8g Fat 7.9 Protein 8.4g

23. Shrimp Cocktail

Preparation Time: 10 minutes Cooking Time: 5 minutes Servings: 1

Ingredients:

4 green onions, chopped 1 lb. cleaned shrimp 1/2cup Miracle Whip Dressing (alternatively you can mix Mayonnaise and Paprika together). 1 dash of Sriracha/hot sauce 20 endive leaves (you can use lettuce/ any sturdy leaf alternative) 1 tbsp. butter 1/2tbsp. garlic paste 1/2tsp lemon juice

Directions

Heat a pan with the butter in it, on medium heat. Once the butter has melted and sizzling, add in your shrimp and garlic paste. Cook for about 5 minutes until the shrimp flesh turns pink. In a separate bowl mix your dressing and lemon juice, and combine the shrimp once cooked and cooled down to room temperature. Wash and separate the endive leaves and plate the leaves facing up - so that they create little bowl-like shapes. Spoon out the shrimp cocktail into the leaves and add a dash of sriracha sauce to each leaf bowl. Nutrition: Calories 196 Carbs 5.8g Fat 11.3g Protein 17.6g

24. Spinach Artichoke Dip

Preparation time: 15 minutes Cooking time: 10 minutes Servings: 4

Ingredients:

Salt and pepper to taste 3 tablespoons butter 3 tablespoons flour 11/2cups milk 1/2teaspoon salt 1/4teaspoon black pepper 5 ounces spinach, frozen and chopped 1/4cup artichokes, diced (I personally like to use marinated) 1/2teaspoon garlic, chopped 1/2cup parmesan, shredded 1/2cup mozzarella, shredded 1 tablespoon asiago cheese, shredded 1 tablespoon romano cheese, shredded 2 tablespoons cream cheese 1/4cup mozzarella cheese (for topping)

Directions

Melt butter over medium heat in a saucepan. Add flour and cook for about 1–2 minutes. Add milk and stir until thick. Season with salt and pepper to taste. Add spinach, diced artichokes, garlic, cheeses, and cream cheese to the pan. Stir until warmed. Pour into a small baking dish. Sprinkle mozzarella cheese on top and place under the broiler. Broil until the top begins browning. Nutrition: Calories 238, Total Fat 15 g, Carbs 12 g, Protein 13 g, Sodium 418 mg

25. Margarita

Preparation Time: 1 minute Cooking Time: 0 minutes Servings 1

Ingredients 11/2ounce of Cuervo or 1800 gold tequila 3/4 ounce of Cointreau 3/4 ounce of Grand Marnier 1/2ounce of lime juice 2 ounces of sour mix Ice, for serving

Directions Refrigerate (or even freeze) the glass you plan to use. While chilling, mix all the ingredients in a shaker and shake well. If you wish salt on your margarita rim, pour some sea salt on a little dish, wet the rim of your chilled glass, and read the salt. Add some ice, and pour the margarita mixture in. Nutrition: Calories: 153 Total Fat: 0g Carbs:7g Protein: 0.2g Fiber:0.2g

26. Pei Wei's Thai Chicken Satay

Preparation Time: 10 minutes Cooking time: 30 minutes Servings: 4

Ingredients: 1-pound boneless, skinless chicken thighs 6-inch bamboo skewers, soaked in water Thai satay marinade 1 tablespoon coriander seeds 1 teaspoon cumin seeds 2 teaspoons chopped lemongrass 1 teaspoon salt 1 teaspoon turmeric powder 1/4teaspoon roasted chili 1/2cup coconut milk 11/2tablespoons light brown sugar 1 teaspoon lime juice 2 teaspoons fish sauce Peanut sauce 2 tablespoons soy sauce 1 tablespoon rice wine vinegar 2 tablespoons brown sugar 1/4cup peanut butter 1 teaspoon chipotle Tabasco Whisk all ingredients until well incorporated. Store in an airtight container in the refrigerator. Will last for 3 days. Thai sweet cucumber relish 1/4cup white vinegar 3/4 cup sugar 3/4 cup water 1 tablespoon ginger, minced 1 Thai red chili, minced 1 medium cucumber 1 tablespoon toasted peanuts, chopped **Directions** Cut any excess fat from the chicken, then cut into strips about 3 inches long and 1 inch wide. Thread the strips onto the skewers. Prepare the Thai Satay Marinade and the Peanut Sauce in separate bowls by simply whisking together all of the ingredients for each. Dip the chicken skewers in the Thai Satay Marinade and allow to marinate for at least 4 hours. Reserve the marinade when you remove the chicken skewers. You can either cook the skewers on the grill, basting with the marinade halfway through, or you can do the same in a 350-degree F oven. They taste better on the grill. To prepare the Cucumber Relish, simply add all of the ingredients together and stir to make sure the cucumber is coated. When the chicken skewers are done cooking, serve with peanut sauce and the cucumber relish. Nutrition: Calories 404, Total Fat 12 g, Carbs 59 g, Protein 8 g, Sodium 436 mg

27. Sweet Corn Cakes

Preparation time: 15 minutes Cooking time 15 minutes Servings: 4

Ingredients:

For the Salsa Verde: 2 tomatillos, roughly chopped 1 (4 -ounce) can diced green chilies, drained 1 green onion, sliced thin 2 tablespoons fresh cilantro, roughly chopped 1 1/2teaspoons granulated sugar 1/4teaspoon ground cumin 1/4teaspoon salt 1/8 teaspoon ground black pepper For the Pico De Gallo: 1 large Roma tomato, diced 1 tablespoon red onion, diced 1 tablespoon fresh cilantro, minced 1/2teaspoon lime juice Salt and ground pepper to taste For Southwestern Sauce: 1/2cup mayonnaise 1 teaspoon white vinegar 1 teaspoon water 1/2teaspoon granulated sugar 1/2teaspoon chili powder 1/4teaspoon paprika 1/8 teaspoon cayenne pepper 1/4teaspoon onion powder 1/8 teaspoon garlic powder For the Corn Cakes: 1 1/2cups frozen sweet corn, divided 1/2cup butter, softened to room temperature 3 tablespoons sugar 1/8 teaspoon salt 1/2cup corn masa harina flour 2 tablespoons all-purpose flour 1 1/2tablespoons olive oil For Garnish: Sour cream Avocado, diced Fresh cilantro, chopped

Directions

First, make the Salsa Verde. Pulse the ingredients for the Salsa Verde in the blender so it is roughly combined. Make the Pico de Gallo and Southwestern Sauce by combining the ingredients together. When they are all well combined, cover them and put them in the refrigerator. Prepare the corn cakes. First, place 1 cup of corn in the blender or food processor and purée. Combine the puréed corn, butter, sugar, salt in a medium bowl, and mix it. In a small bowl, combine the masa and flour and stir. Add the remaining corn and masa mixture to the butter and corn mixture and then form into patties. Heat the oil in a large skillet over medium-low to medium heat. When oil is hot, add the corn cakes and fry on each side for about 5 to 8 minutes. Serve with the salsa Verde, Pico de Gallo and Southwestern sauce for dipping. Garnish with sour cream, avocado, and cilantro. Nutrition: Calories: 320 Fat: 16.6 g Carbs: 30. 1 g Protein: 21.6 g Sodium: 452 mg

28. Olive Garden Bread Sticks

Preparation time: 5 minutes Cooking time: 15 minutes Servings: 6

Ingredients: 1 (10.5 ounce/6 count) package frozen bread sticks 2 tablespoons olive oil 1/4cup Parmesan cheese

Directions Preheat oven to 350°F. Brush each bread sticks with olive oil. Sprinkle the tops of the bread with Parmesan cheese. Wrap in aluminum foil. Bake for 12–15 minutes, according to package directions. Dipping Sauces: Olive Garden also serves dipping sauces for an extra charge. To get the restaurant feel, place some warm bowls of marinara and Alfredo sauce on the table to dip the bread sticks into. Nutrition: Calories 14 Carbs 1.5g Fat 0.8 Protein 0.5g

29. Veg Samosas

Preparation Time: 20 minutes Cooking Time: 20 minutes Servings: 4

Ingredients: 1 potato, peeled & cubed 2 tbsps. of oil 1 onion, finely chopped 3/4 cups of frozen peas & carrots 1 tsp of garam masala 1/2tsp curry powder 1/2tsp turmeric 1 curry leaf 1/2tsp of mustard seeds salt to taste 1 sheet of frozen puff pastry (leave it at room temperature for an hour before cooking so that it can defrost)

Directions Preheat the oven to 400°F. Fill a small pot with water and bring to a boil. Add the potatoes into the pot and lower the heat to medium-low. Let it simmer for 15 minutes until potatoes are soft. In a medium pan over medium heat, drizzle a dash of oil in it and add your onions, masala, curry powder, salt, turmeric, curry leaf and mustard seeds. Fry for about 3 minutes until the onions have browned. Incorporate the peas, carrots, peas and potato into the pan with the onions and cook for another 3 minutes, stirring lightly to mix all the spices. You will get a marvelous aroma of spices as you thoroughly mix the contents. Lightly cover your counter area with some flour and get a bowl of water ready, with a pastry brush ready. Line an oven tray with parchment paper and keep it aside. Lay your pastry on the flour covered countertop and cut it into 9 equally sized rectangles. Fold over one corner of the rectangle to touch the rectangle's bottom, creating a cone-like shape. Add a tablespoon of potato filling into the cone shape and then lightly brush the remaining bit of pastry with water. Fold over the remaining pastry around the filling, creating a triangular shape. Repeat for the rest of the samosas. Pop the tray in the oven and bake for 15 minutes. Nutrition: Calories 153 Carbs 12.9g Fat 7.8 Protein 2g

30. Toasted Ravioli

Preparation time: 10 minutes Cooking time: 10 minutes Servings: 4–6

Ingredients:

1 (1-pound) package meat ravioli, thawed 2 eggs 1/4cup water 1 teaspoon garlic salt 1 cup flour 1 cup breadcrumbs 1/2teaspoon oregano 1 teaspoon basil Grated parmesan (for garnish)

Directions

Add the eggs and water to a small bowl. Beat together. To another bowl, add the oregano, basil, garlic salt, and bread crumbs. Combine together. To a third bowl, add the flour. Heat oil to 350°F. Dip the ravioli in the flour, then the eggs, then the breadcrumbs. Repeat for each and set aside. Place in oil and fry until golden brown. Place on a cooling rack or paper towel to drain some of the oil. If desired, sprinkle with parmesan. Serve with marinara sauce. Nutrition: Calories 228, Total Fat 15 g, Carbs 12 g, Protein 13 g, Sodium 418 mg

31. Burrito

Preparation Time: 15 minutes Cooking Time: 20 minutes Servings: 10

Ingredients: 1 pound pork sausage mild 1/2 cup yellow onion diced 1/4 cup fresh tomatoes diced   One tablespoon of green chilies 10 — tortillas Nine eggs 6 ounces American cheese 12 sliced pieces 1/2 cup salsa

Directions Crumble and fry the pork sausage, stir and break the meat in small parts to cook.   Place drained sausage in the frying pan. Add the onion, green chilies and tomatoes, heat up at medium temperature until sausage and vegetables are cooked through. Stir from time to time. Measure and beat 2 cups of eggs. Add the eggs and the sausage mixture to the pan. When finished, take off from the heat. Then place sausages and egg mixture (2 tablespoons) on one tortilla. Break each slice of American cheese into two even portions, then put the cheese onto the sausage mixture, and roll the tortilla. If you do all of these ahead of time, you can wrap them in plastic to put them in the refrigerator or freezer, and then heat them for a moment or two in the microwave. Serve with the taco or picante sauce, as you like. You will find these are milder for breakfast and very significant.   Nutrition Calories: 269 kcal, Carbohydrates: 3 g, Protein: 15 g, Fat: 21 g, Saturated Fat: 8 g, Cholesterol: 196

32. Applebee's Triple Chocolate Meltdown

Preparation time:

25 minutes Cooking time: 8 minutes Servings: 2–3 **Ingredients** 4 ounces semisweet chocolate chips 1/2cup butter 2 large whole eggs 2 large egg yolks 1/4cup sugar, plus more for dusting 2 tablespoons of all-purpose flour 1/4teaspoon salt Toppings 4 ounces white chocolate 4 ounces semisweet chocolate 2 teaspoons vegetable shortening, divided 4 scoops vanilla ice cream

Directions

Preheat oven to 400°F. Grease muffin pans or ramekins and mud with sugar. Melt chocolate chips with butter over a double saucepan, whisking until smooth. In a separate bowl, whisk together the entire eggs, yolks, and sugar until light and fluffy. Whisk both mixtures together. Gradually add flour and salt, whisking until blended. Distribute evenly into prepared pans and arrange on a baking sheet. Bake until edges are done, and centers are still soft (about 8 minutes). Invert onto plate. Prepare toppings. Place each sort of chocolate in separate, microwave-safe bowls. Add a teaspoon of shortening to every bowl and cook in the microwave for about 15 seconds and stir. Repeat until smooth. Top the cake pieces with frozen dessert and drizzle with melted chocolate. Nutrition Calories 727, Total Fat 31 g, Carbohydrates 107 g, Protein 11 g, Sodium 562 mg

33. Pei Wei's Vietnamese Chicken Salad Spring Roll

Preparation Time: 10 minutes Cooking time: 5 minutes Servings: 6

Ingredients:

Salad Rice Wrappers Green leaf lettuce like Boston Bibb lettuce Napa cabbage, shredded Green onions, chopped Mint, chopped Carrots, cut into 1-inch matchsticks Peanuts Chicken, diced and cooked, about 6 chicken tenders drizzled with soy sauce, honey, garlic powder, and red pepper flakes Lime dressing 2 tablespoons lime juice, about 1 lime 11/2teaspoons water 1 tablespoon sugar 1 teaspoon salt Dash of pepper 3 tablespoons oil Add everything but the oil to a small container or bowl and shake or stir until the sugar and salt are dissolved. Then, add the oil and shake well. Peanut dipping sauce 2 tablespoons soy sauce 1 tablespoon rice wine vinegar 2 tablespoons brown sugar 1/4cup peanut butter 1 teaspoon chipotle Tabasco 1 teaspoon honey 1 teaspoon sweet chili sauce   1 teaspoon lime vinaigrette Add all the ingredients to a small bowl and mix to combine thoroughly.

Directions

In a large bowl, mix together all of the salad ingredients except for the rice wrappers and lettuce. Place the rice wrappers in warm water for about 1 minute to soften. Transfer the wrappers to a plate and top each with 2 pieces of lettuce. Top the lettuce with the salad mixture and drizzle with the lime dressing. Fold the wrapper by tucking in the ends and then rolling. Serve with lime dressing and peanut dipping sauce. Nutrition: Calories 218, Total Fat 24 g, Carbs 14 g, Protein 17 g,

PASTA AND SOUPS RECIPES

34. Bob Evan's Hearty Beef Vegetable Soup

Preparation Time:20 minutes Cooking Time: 11 hours 10minutes Servings: 5

Ingredients: 1-pound beef, lean ground 1 onion, chopped 1/2 tsp. salt 1/4 tsp. pepper 2 1/2 cups water 3 potatoes, and cut into cubes 1 can Italian diced tomatoes, 1 cup celery 1 cup carrots 2 tbsp. sugar 1 tbsp. dried parsley flakes 2 tsp. dried basil 1 bay leaf

Directions

Cook onion and beef in a non-stick skillet over medium heat until meat is no longer pink, and split meat into crumbles; rinse. Season with salt and pepper. Shift Slow-cooking. Add ingredients left over. Cover and simmer for 10-11 hours or until vegetables are soft. Dispose of a bay leaf before serving. Nutrition: Calories 218, Total Fat 24 g, Carbs 14 g, Protein 17 g, Bob

35. El Chico's Albondiga Soup

Preparation Time: 20 minutes Cooking Time: 1 hour Servings: 6

Ingredients For the Meatballs (albondigas) 2 slices white bread 1/2cup milk 1 1/2pounds ground beef 1/3 cup dry long-grain rice 2 eggs 1 1/2teaspoons salt 2 teaspoons black pepper For the Soup (sopa) 2 tablespoons vegetable oil 1 onion, diced 1 small bell pepper, diced 3 cloves garlic, chopped 3 quarts water 3 tomatoes, diced 1 cup dry rice 2 tablespoons salt 1 tablespoon cumin 1 tablespoon black pepper 3 carrots, thinly sliced 1 small zucchini, thinly sliced Other Ingredients Cilantro Corn tortilla strips Fresh limes, cut in wedges

Directions Prepare the meatballs. Preheat the oven to 400°F and line a baking tray with foil. Soak the bread slices in the milk for 5–10 minutes. Add the rest of the meatball ingredients and mix to incorporate. Roll the meat mixture into 1-inch balls and arrange them on the baking tray. Bake for 20 minutes and drain on paper towels. Prepare the soup. Heat the oil in a large soup pot or Dutch oven. Sauté the onion and pepper until they begin to sweat and soften, about 5 minutes. Add the garlic and cook 1 more minute. Add the water, tomatoes, rice, and seasonings. Bring the pot to a boil, and then carefully add the meatballs, carrots, and zucchini. Simmer until the rice is soft, about 30 minutes. To serve, garnish with cilantro and tortilla strips. Squeeze lime juice over the bowls. Nutrition: Calories 221 Carbs 2 g Fat 8.2 g Protein 12 g

36. Cheesecake Factory's Pasta di Vinci

Preparation Time: 10 minutes Cooking Time: 50 minutes Servings: 4

Ingredients: 1/2red onion, chopped 1 cup mushrooms, quartered 2 teaspoons garlic, chopped 1-pound chicken breast, cut into bite-size pieces 3 tablespoons butter, divided 2 tablespoons flour 2 teaspoons salt 1/4cup white wine 1 cup cream of chicken soup mixed with some milk 4 tablespoons heavy cream Basil leaves for serving, chopped Parmesan cheese for serving 1 pound penne pasta, cooked, drained

Directions

Sauté the onion, mushrooms and garlic in 1 tablespoon of the butter. When they are tender, remove them from the butter and place in a bowl. Cook the chicken in the same pan. When the chicken is done, transfer it to the bowl containing the garlic, onions, and mushrooms, and set everything aside. Using the same pan, make a roux using the flour and remaining butter over low to medium heat. When the roux is ready, mix in the salt, wine, and cream of chicken mixture. Continue stirring the mixture, making sure that it does not burn. When the mixture thickens, allow the mixture to simmer for a few more minutes. Mix in the ingredients that you set aside and transfer the cooked pasta to a bowl or plate. Pour the sauce over the pasta, garnish with parmesan cheese and basil, and serve. Nutrition: Calories 218, Total Fat 24 g, Carbs 14 g, Protein 17 g,

37. Panera Creamy Tomato Soup

Preparation Time: 10 minutes Cooking Time: 15 minutes Servings: 3

Ingredients: 2 tbsp. olive oil 1 cup white onions, chopped 2 tsp. garlic, minced 60 ounces' tomato puree 2 tsp. basil, dried 1/2 tsp. oregano 15 ounces' vegetable stock 1/2 cup cream 1 tsp. sugar Salt to taste Black pepper to taste

Directions In a saucepan, add olive oil and heat over medium heat and chopped white onion. Sprinkle of salt on top. Sauté until transparent to the onions. Add the chopped garlic and sauté until fragrant. Tomatoes puree, basil, vegetable stock, oregano, and heavy cream are added. Reduce to simmer oil. Simmer for 9-10 minutes. Nice taste, and apply sugar if the soup is too acid. You can make puree soup with either an electric mixer or in a blender. Season it with salt and black pepper. Nutrition: Calories: 361 Fat: 44.9 g Carbs: 85. 6 g Protein: 16.8 g Sodium: 494 mg

38. California Pizza Kitchen's Kung Pao Spaghetti

Preparation Time: 10 minutes Cooking time 10 minutes Servings 4–6

Ingredients

1 cup of chicken stock 4 tablespoons of cornstarch, divided 3/4 cup of soy sauce 1/2cup of sherry 3 tablespoons of chili paste with garlic 1/4cup of sugar 2 tablespoons of red wine vinegar 2 tablespoons of sesame oil 2 egg whites 1/2teaspoon of salt 1-pound of spaghetti 1/4cup of olive oil 1-pound of boneless skinless chicken breast, cut into 3/4-inch cubes 10–15 whole Chinese dried red chili peppers; DO NOT eat them for color and heat! 1 cup of unsalted dry roasted peanuts 1/4cup garlic, minced 3 cups green onions, greens, and white parts, coarsely chopped

Directions

Make the sauce by whisking together the chicken broth and a couple of tablespoons of cornstarch. Stir until the cornstarch dissolves. Whisk in the soy, sherry, chili paste, sugar, vinegar, and vegetable oil. Bring back a boil. Turn the warmth down and simmer until the sauce thickens about 20 minutes. In a small bowl, whisk together the egg whites, two tablespoons of cornstarch, and salt. Stir until well blended, but not such a lot that the egg whites froth. Bring salted water to a quick boil in a large pot. Add the pasta and cook until almost hard. Drain. Heat the vegetable oil in a large skillet over medium-high heat. Add the cut chicken pieces to the albumen mixture and stir to coat. Carefully add the chicken and albumen mixture to the skillet to make a "pancake." Cook until the egg sets, then flip and cook on the opposite side. Separate the chicken pieces. When the chicken pieces turn golden brown, stir in the garlic and scallions and cook for about 30 seconds. Add the sauce that you simply made earlier and go to ensure it covers everything. Add the pasta and stir to mix with the sauce. Nutrition: Calories: 890, Total Fat: 37g, Carbs: 112g, Protein: 28g, Fiber:9g

39. Macaroni Grill's Pasta Milano

Preparation Time: 5 minutes Cooking Time: 20 minutes Servings: 6

Ingredients:

1 pound bowtie pasta 2 teaspoons olive oil 1 pound chicken, chopped into small pieces 1 12-ounce package mushrooms, chopped 1 cup onion, minced 2 garlic cloves, finely minced 1/2cup sun dried tomatoes, diced 11/2cups half and half 1 tablespoon butter, softened 1/2cup Parmesan cheese, shredded, plus some more for serving 1 teaspoon black pepper, ground 1 tablespoon fresh basil, minced

Directions

Follow instructions on package to cook bowtie pasta. Drain, then set aside. Add oil to a pan over medium-high heat. Once hot, add chicken and stir-fry for about 5 to 6 minutes until cooked through. Set chicken aside onto a plate. In the same pan, toss in mushrooms, onions, garlic, and sun dried tomatoes. Sauté until onions turn soft and mushrooms become a light brown, then sprinkle salt and pepper to season. Return chicken to pan and mix. Mix half and half, butter, Parmesan, pepper, and basil in a small bowl. Add half and half mixture to pan. Stir, and let simmer for about 3 to 4 minutes or until pan ingredients are thoroughly heated. Mix in pasta until coated well. Serve. Nutrition: Calories 218, Total Fat 14 g, Carbs 11 g,

40. Chicken Noodle Soup

Preparation Time: 5 minutes Cooking Time: 4 hours 15 minutes Servings: 6

Ingredients: 2 boneless, skinless chicken breasts 1 cup egg noodles 2 cups water or as required onion, small, diced 2 cans chicken broth 1 teaspoon thyme 2 cups celery, diced 1 bay leaf 2 cups carrots, diced 1 teaspoon minced garlic or garlic Pepper and salt to taste

Directions: Place the entire ingredients (except the egg noodles) in the bottom of your crock pot; give everything a good stir until evenly combined. Cover & cook for 3 to 4 hours on high-heat or 6 to 8 hours on low-heat. Just 30 minutes before you serve this soup, remove the chicken pieces & shred. Place them to the pot again. Turn on the high of your crock pot & add in the egg noodles; let cook for half an hour. Serve immediately and enjoy. Nutrition: Calories: 124 Total Fat: 4.7g Cholesterol: 25mg Sodium: 1731mg Potassium: 109mg Carbohydrates: 15g

41. Three Cheese Chicken Penne from Applebee's

Preparation Time: 10 minutes Cooking Time: 1 hour Servings: 4

Ingredients:

2 boneless skinless chicken breasts   1 cup Italian salad dressing   3 cups penne pasta   6 tablespoons olive oil, divided   15 ounces Alfredo sauce   8 ounces combination mozzarella, Parmesan, and provolone cheeses, grated   4 roma tomatoes, seeded and diced   4 tablespoons fresh basil, diced   2 cloves garlic, finely chopped   Shredded parmesan cheese for serving

Directions:

Preheat oven to 350°F.   In a bowl, add chicken then drizzle with Italian dressing. Mix to coat chicken with dressing fully. Cover using plastic wrap and keep inside refrigerator overnight but, if you're in a hurry, at least 2 hours is fine.   Follow instructions on package to cook penne pasta. Drain, then set aside.   Brush 3 tablespoons oil onto grates of grill then preheat to medium-high heat. Add marinated chicken onto grill, discarding the marinade. Cook chicken until both sides are fully cooked and internal temperature measures 165°F. Remove from grill. Set aside until cool enough to handle. Then, cut chicken into thin slices.   In a large bowl, add cooked noodles, Alfredo sauce, and grilled chicken. Mix until combined.   Drizzle remaining oil onto large casserole pan, then pour noodle mixture inside. Sprinkle cheeses on top. Bake for about 15-20 minutes or until cheese turns a golden and edges of mixture begins to bubble. Remove from oven.   Mix tomatoes, basil, and garlic in a bowl. Add on top of pasta.   Sprinkle parmesan cheese before serving.   Nutrition: Calories 308, Total Fat 34 g, Carbs 18 g, Protein 17 g,

42. Spaghetti Frittata

Preparation Time: 5 minutes Cooking Time: 30 minutes Servings: 6

Ingredients:

1/2cup chopped green pepper or 1/2cup chopped onion   2 tablespoons olive oil   1 tablespoon butter   1/4cup milk   2 cups grated Parmesan cheese   1/2teaspoon dried basil leaves   1 cup cooked spaghetti or fettuccine cut into 5 cm pieces   6 eggs

Directions:

Heat the olive oil and butter in a pan until it melts.   Add the green pepper and cook over medium heat, stirring frequently until tender and crispy at the same time.   Meanwhile, in a large bowl, mix the eggs with the milk, 1/4cup grated Parmesan cheese, salt and pepper, and basil.   Add the cooked pasta to the egg mixture and stir gently.   Next, add the egg mixture to the pan and arrange the pasta in a uniform layer.   Cook the egg mixture over medium heat, raising the sides with a spatula occasionally so that the raw egg flows underneath.   When the egg mixture is almost ready, but still moist, after 10 minutes, cover it with grated Parmesan cheese. Cook for a few more minutes until it begins to brown. Remove from the oven and cut the frittata into pieces. Serve immediately.   Nutrition: Calories 350, Total Fat 24 g, Carbs 14 g, Protein 17 g,

43. Chicken Enchilada Soup from Chili's

Preparation Time: 10 minutes Cooking Time: 50 minutes Servings: 8

Ingredients

1-pound of chicken breast, boneless and skinless, cut in half 1 tablespoon of vegetable oil 1/2cup of onion, chopped 1 garlic clove, finely chopped 1-quart chicken broth 1 cup of masa harina 3 cups of water, divided 1 cup of enchilada sauce 2 cups of cheddar cheese, grated 1 teaspoon of salt 1 teaspoon of chili powder 1/2teaspoon of ground cumin Crispy tortilla strips for garnish

Directions

Heat oil in a pot over medium heat. Add chicken breasts and evenly cook until browned on all sides. Remove from pot. Shred, then put aside. Return pot to heat and add onion and garlic. Sauté until onions are translucent. Add chicken stock. Mix masa harina and a couple of cups water in a bowl, then add in the pot with the onions and garlic. Add the remaining water, enchilada sauce, cheddar, salt, flavorer, and cumin. Bring mixture to a boil. Add cooked chicken to the pot and lower heat. Simmer for about 30 to 40 minutes until soup is thick. Garnish with crispy tortilla strips and serve. Nutrition: Calories: 290, Total fat: 16 g, Saturated fat: 9 g, Carbs: 14 g, Sugar: 1 g, Fibers: 2 g, Protein: 22 g, Sodium: 512 mg

44. Macaroni and Cheese

Preparation Time: 10 minutes Cooking time: 30 minutes Servings: 3

Ingredients: 2 tablespoons butter 2 tablespoons flour 1 teaspoon salt 1 teaspoon dry mustard 21/2cups milk 1/2pound (about 2 cups) cheddar (divided) 1/2pound (2 cups) elbow macaroni, cooked

Directions:

Preheat the oven to 375°F. Melt the butter in a saucepan, then stir in the flour, salt, and mustard. Whisk in the milk and stir constantly until the sauce begins to thicken. Stir in 11/2cups of the cheese. Continue to stir until melted, then remove from the heat. Add the cooked elbow macaroni and the cheese sauce to a buttered casserole dish. Stir until the macaroni is covered with sauce. Top with the remaining cheese and bake for 25 minutes or until the top is browned and the cheese is bubbly. Nutrition: Calories 115 Protein 35 Carbs 26 Fat 5

45. Evan's Cheddar Baked Potato Soup

Preparation Time: 10 minutes Cooking Time: 35 minutes Servings: 1

Ingredients: 1 can Campbell's Cheddar Cheese Soup 1 can chicken broth 1-pound Cheddar Cheese 4 cups whole milk   2 tbsp. butter 2 tbsp. Corn Starch 1/2 tsp. Salt 1/2 tsp. Pepper 1/2 tsp. Onion powder   1/2 tsp. Garlic salt   7 potatoes, diced and boiled

Directions Add soup, bread, 1 milk, and stir. Garnish with cheese and milk. With the rest of the broth, stir in cornstarch, add to soup. Add extra spices and butter. Bring to a boil, lower heat, and cook for 15-20 minutes. Add boiled potatoes, then cook for another 15 minutes. Top with peppers and chives bits' bacon. Let it cool and reheat for the best taste. Nutrition: Calories: 452 Fat: 19.1 g Carbs: 15. 5 g Protein: 23.5 g Sodium: 250 mg

46. Cajun Chicken Pasta from Chili's

Preparation Time: 10 minutes Cooking Time: 20 minutes Servings: 4

Ingredients: 2 chicken breasts, boneless and skinless 1 tablespoon olive oil, divided 1 tablespoon Cajun seasoning 3 quarts' water 1/2tablespoon salt 8 ounces' penne pasta 2 tablespoons unsalted butter 3 garlic cloves, minced 1 cup heavy cream 1/2teaspoon lemon zest 1/4cup Parmesan cheese, shredded Salt and black pepper, to taste 1 tablespoon oil 2 Roma tomatoes, diced 2 tablespoons parsley chopped

Directions

Place chicken in a Ziploc bag. Add 1 tablespoon oil and Cajun seasoning. Using your hands, combine chicken and mixture until well-coated. Seal tightly and set aside to marinate. Cook pasta in a pot filled with salt and boiling water. Follow package instructions. Drain and set aside. In a skillet, heat butter over medium heat. Sauté garlic for 1 minute or until aromatic. Slowly add cream, followed by lemon zest. Cook for 1 minute, stirring continuously until fully blended. Toss in Parmesan cheese. Mix until sauce is a little thick, then add salt and pepper. Add pasta and combine until well-coated. Transfer onto a bowl and keep warm. In a separate skillet, heat remaining oil. Cook chicken over medium-high heat for about 5 minutes on each side or until fully cooked through. Transfer onto chopping board and cut into thin strips. Top pasta with chicken and sprinkle with tomatoes and parsley on top. Serve. Nutrition: Calories 655 Total Fat 38 g Carbs 47 g Protein 31 g Sodium 359 mg

47. Macaroni Grill Pasta Milano Soup

Preparation Time: 15 minutes Cooking Time: 25 minutes Servings: 3

Ingredients:

2 tbsp. butter 1 yellow onion, diced clove garlic, minced 2 tbsp. Gold Medal all-purpose flour 2 cups Progresso chicken broth 2 jars Alfredo sauce 1 cup whole milk 1/4cup heavy cream   2 cups grilled chicken strips, pre-cooked 2 cans sliced mushrooms 1 can Muir Glen organic fire-roasted tomatoes   1/2 cup oil-packed sun-dried tomatoes, chopped 2 tbsp. fresh parsley Salt and pepper to taste 2 cups cooked bowtie pasta

Directions

Melt the butter over medium heat in an oven or stockpot, and cook the onions and garlic until soft and translucent for about 5 minutes. Remove the rice and mix to blend. Add the broth, Alfredo sauce, milk, and heavy cream and combine to stir. Boost the heat and bring it to a boil, frequently stirring until the sauce has thickened slightly. Add the grilled chicken, sun-dried tomatoes, and mushrooms. Stir to merge. Let it boil, reduce the heat to medium-low and simmer, covered for 15 minutes. Add the bowtie pasta and the parsley. Stir to mix for another 2 minutes, and simmer. Season with salt and pepper. Nutrition: Calories: 441 Fat: 7.2 g Carbs: 12. 3 g Protein: 5.8 g Sodium: 213 mg

48. Red Lobster's Shrimp Pasta

Preparation Time: 5 minutes Cooking Time: 30 minutes Servings: 4

Ingredients 8 ounces of linguini or spaghetti pasta 1/3 cup of extra virgin olive oil 3 garlic cloves 1-pound of shrimp, peeled, deveined 2/3 cup of clam juice or chicken broth 1/3 cup of white wine 1 cup of heavy cream 1/2cup of Parmesan cheese, freshly grated 1/4teaspoon of dried basil, crushed 1/4teaspoon of dried oregano, crushed Fresh parsley and Parmesan cheese for garnish

Directions

Cook the Pasta consistent with package directions. Simmer the garlic in hot oil over low heat until tender. Increase the warmth from low to medium and add the shrimp. When the shrimp is cooked, transfer it to a separate bowl alongside the garlic. Keep the remaining oil in the pan. Pour the clam or chicken stock into the pan and convey it to a boil. Add the wine and adjust the warmth to medium. Keep cooking the mixture for an additional 3 minutes. While stirring the mixture, reduce the warmth to low and add in the cream and cheese. Keep stirring. When the mixture thickens, return the shrimp to the pan and contribute the remaining ingredients (except the pasta). Place the pasta in a bowl and pour the sauce over it. Mix and serve. Garnish with parsley and parmesan cheese, if desired Nutrition: Calories: 590, Total Fat: 26 g, Carbs: 54 g, Protein: 34 g, Sodium: 1500 mg

49. Chow Mein from Panda Express

Preparation Time: 5 minutes Cooking Time: 30 minutes Servings: 6

Ingredients: 8 quarts water 12 ounces Yakisoba noodles 1/4cup soy sauce 3 garlic cloves, finely chopped 1 tablespoon brown sugar 2 teaspoons ginger, grated 1/4teaspoon white pepper, ground 2 tablespoons olive oil 1 onion, finely chopped 3 celery stalks, sliced on the bias 2 cups cabbage, chopped

Directions In a pot, bring water to a boil. Cook Yakisoba noodles for about 1 minute until noodles separate. Drain and set aside. Combine soy sauce, garlic, brown sugar, ginger, and white pepper in a bowl. In a pan, heat oil on medium-high heat. Sauté onion and celery for 3 minutes or until soft. Add cabbage and stir-fry for an additional minute. Mix in noodles and soy sauce mixture. Cook for 2 minutes, stirring continuously until noodles are well-coated. Transfer into bowls. Serve. Nutrition: Calories 218, Total Fat 24 g, Carbs 14 g, Protein 17 g,

50. Pesto Chicken and Broccoli Pasta

Preparation Time: 15 minutes Cooking Time: 30 minutes Servings: 4

Ingredients:

4 cups cooked pasta 1/2onion, minced 4 garlic cloves, minced 1/4cup pesto 2 chicken breasts; sliced into ½" strips 1 cup half and half or light cream 1/4cup parmesan cheese, grated 1 cup broccoli florets, fresh or frozen 1/4teaspoon pepper or to taste 1 tablespoon olive oil 1/2teaspoon salt

Directions:

Cook the pasta in a large pot per the directions mentioned on the package. During the last one minute of your cooking; add broccoli into the pot with pasta. Drain & set aside until ready to use. In the meantime, over moderate heat in a large pan; heat 1 tablespoon of oil. Add and cook the onion until turn golden, for 3 to 4 minutes. Add and cook the garlic for a couple of seconds and then add the sliced chicken. Season with pepper & salt; cook until the chicken turn browned, for 5 to 7 minutes. Add the cream, parmesan, pesto, pepper & salt. Let the mixture to simmer for 2 to 3 minutes. Add the cooked broccoli and pasta. Give the ingredients a good stir until completely combined. Let simmer for 2 to 3 more minutes. Remove from heat & garnish with additional parmesan. Serve hot & enjoy. Nutrition: Calories 318, Total Fat 24 g, Carbs 14 g, Protein 17 g,

51. Pesto Cavatappi from Noodles & Company

Preparation Time: 5 minutes Cooking Time: 20 minutes Servings: 8

Ingredients: 4 quarts water 1 tablespoon salt 1-pound macaroni pasta 1 teaspoon olive oil 1 large tomato, finely chopped 4 ounces mushrooms, finely chopped 1/4cup chicken broth 1/4cup dry white wine 1/4cup heavy cream 1 cup pesto 1 cup Parmesan cheese, grated

Directions: Add water and salt to a pot. Bring to a boil. Put in pasta and cook for 10 minutes or until al dente. Drain and set aside. In a pan, heat oil. Sauté tomatoes and mushrooms for 5 minutes. Pour in broth, wine, and cream. Bring to a boil. Reduce heat to medium and simmer for 2 minutes or until mixture is thick. Stir in pesto and cook for another 2 minutes. Toss in pasta. Mix until fully coated. Transfer onto plates and sprinkle with Parmesan cheese. Nutrition: Calories 289, Total Fat 24 g, Carbs 13 g, Protein 17 g,

52. Olive Garden's Fettuccine Alfredo

Preparation Time: 5 minutes Cooking Time: 25 minutes Servings: 6

Ingredients:

1/2cup butter, melted   2 tablespoons cream cheese   1 pint heavy cream 1 teaspoon garlic powder   Some salt   Some black pepper   2/3 cup parmesan cheese, grated   1 pound fettuccine, cooked

Directions:

Melt the cream cheese in the melted butter over medium heat until soft. Add the heavy cream and season the mixture with garlic powder, salt, and pepper. Reduce the heat to low and allow the mixture to simmer for another 15 to 20 minutes. Remove the mixture from heat and add in the parmesan. Stir everything to melt the cheese. Pour the sauce over the pasta and serve. Nutrition: Calories 330, Total Fat 29 g, Carbs 34 g, Protein 12 g,

53. Outback's Baked Potato Soup

Preparation Time: 5 minutes Cooking Time: 40 minutes Servings: 8

Ingredients

2 quarts water 8 medium-sized potatoes, cut into chunks 4 cans of chicken broth 1 small onion, minced 1 teaspoon salt 1 teaspoon of ground pepper 2 cups of cold water 1 cup of butter 3/4 cup of flour 11/2cup of heavy cream 11/2cups of jack cheese 2-3 thick-cut bacon slices, cooked and diced 1/4cup of green onion, minced

Directions

In a pot, add water and potatoes. Bring back a boil, reduce heat to medium, and cook potatoes for 10-15 minutes or tender. Drain and put aside. In a separate pot, pour in broth and blend in onions, salt, pepper, and water. Simmer for 20 minutes. Meanwhile, in another pot, whisk together butter and flour. Slowly add this to the pan of broth. Stir in cream to the mixture and simmer for 20 minutes. Mix in potatoes to reheat. Sprinkle jack cheese, bacon bits, and green onions on top. Serve. Nutrition: Calories: 845, Total Fat: 49 g, Carbs: 81 g, Protein: 23 g, Sodium: 1652 mg

54. Disneyland's Monterey Clam Chowder

Preparation Time: 15 minutes Cooking Time: 1 hour Servings: 4

Ingredients

5 tablespoons of butter 5 tablespoons of flour 2 tablespoons of vegetable oil 11/2cups of potatoes (peeled, diced) 1/2cup of onion, diced 1/2cup of red pepper 1/2cup of green pepper 1/2cup of celery 21/4cups of clam juice 11/2cups of heavy cream 1 cup of clams, chopped 1 tablespoon of fresh thyme or 1/2tablespoon of dried thyme 1/4–1/2teaspoon of salt 1 pinch of white pepper 1/3 –1/2teaspoon of Tabasco sauce 4 individual sourdough of round bread made into bowls Chives for garnish (optional)

Directions

Make a roux by mixing melted butter and flour over medium heat for 10 minutes. Flour burns quickly, so confirm to observe the mixture closely. Set the roux aside. Sauté the potatoes, onions, pepper, and celery in the oil for 10 minutes employing a soup pot. Whisk the other the ingredients, including the roux, into the soup pot, and convey the whole mixture to a boil. After the mixture has boiled, reduce the warmth and let it simmer for an additional 5 minutes. Season the soup as you wish with salt and pepper. To serve, ladle the soup evenly into the prepared bread bowls and sprinkle with fresh chives if desired. Nutrition: Calories: 472.3, Total Fat: 36.9 g, Carbs: 27.4 g, Protein: 9.3 g, Sodium: 771.5 mg

SIDES AND SALADS RECIPES

55. Cinnamon Apples

Preparation Time: 10 minutes Cooking time: 10 minutes Servings: 3

Ingredients:

1/4cup butter 1/2cup apple cider 1 tablespoon cornstarch 2 pounds Golden Delicious apples, cored, peeled and cut into wedges 1 teaspoon lemon juice 1 teaspoon cinnamon 1/8 teaspoon nutmeg 1/8 teaspoon allspice 1/4cup brown sugar

Directions:

In a large skillet, melt your butter over a medium to medium-low heat. Add the apples in a single layer, then top with the lemon juice followed by the brown sugar and spices. Cover, reduce the heat to low, and allow the apples to simmer until tender. Transfer the apples from the skillet to a serving bowl, leaving the juices in the skillet. Whisk 1/2cup of the juice together with the cornstarch in a small bowl. Turn the heat under the skillet up to medium-high and whisk the cornstarch mixture into the rest of the juices. Stir constantly until it thickens and there are no lumps. Pour the juice over the bowl of apples and stir to coat. Nutrition: Calories 115 Protein 35 Carbs 26 Fat 5

56. Brussels Sprout N' Kale Salad

Preparation Time: 10 minutes Cooking time: 1 minutes Servings: 3

Ingredients:

1 bunch kale 1 pound Brussels sprouts 1/4cup craisins (or dry cranberries) 1/2cup pecans, chopped   Maple vinaigrette 1/2cup olive oil 1/4cup apple cider vinegar 1/4cup maple syrup 1 teaspoon dry mustard Directions Slice the kale and Brussels sprouts with a cheese grater or mandolin slicer. Transfer to a salad bowl. Add the pecans to a skillet on high heat. Toast for 60 seconds, then transfer to the salad bowl. Add the craisins. Mix all of the ingredients for the vinaigrette and whisk to combine. Pour the vinaigrette over the salad and toss. Refrigerate for a few hours or preferably overnight before serving. Nutrition: Calories 135 Protein 35 Carbs 26 Fat 5 Tomato, Cucumber and Onion Salad Preparation Time: 10 minutes Cooking time: 0 minutes Servings: 3 Ingredients: 1 pound grape tomatoes 3 cucumbers, sliced 1/2cup white onion, sliced thinly 1 cup white vinegar 2 tablespoons Italian dressing 1/2cup sugar

Directions:

Whisk together the vinegar, sugar, and Italian dressing in a small bowl. Add the cucumbers, tomatoes, and onions. Toss to coat. Cover with plastic wrap and refrigerate until ready to serve or for at least 1 hour before serving. Nutrition: Calories 218, Total Fat 90 g, Carbs 66 g, Protein 39 g, Sodium 2038 mg

57. Pinto Beans

Preparation Time: 10 minutes Cooking time: 60 minutes Servings: 4

Ingredients: 1 pound ham hocks or country ham 1 tablespoon sugar 2 quarts water 2 cups dry pinto beans, sorted and washed 11/2teaspoons salt

Directions: Cook the ham hocks until well done. Reserve the stock and pull the meat from the bone. Remove any pebbles from the beans, rinse them, and add them to a large pot with the water. Season with salt and add the ham and reserved stock. Bring to a boil, then reduce heat, cover and simmer for about 3 hours or until beans are tender. Alternatively, you can add all of the ingredients (with the ham still on the bone) to a slow cooker and cook on low for 6–8 hours. Nutrition: Calories 218, Total Fat 90 g, Carbs 66 g, Protein 39 g, Sodium 2038 mg

58. Dry Garlic Ribs

Preparation Time: 15 minutes Cooking Time: 2 hours 30 minutes Servings: 6

Ingredients:

6 pounds' pork ribs, silver skin removed and cut into individual ribs 11/2cups broth 11/2cups brown sugar 1/4cup soy sauce 12 cloves garlic, minced 1/4cup yellow mustard 1 large onion, finely chopped 1/4teaspoon salt 1/2teaspoon black pepper

Directions:

Preheat oven to 200°F. Season ribs with salt and pepper and place on a baking tray. Cover with aluminum foil and bake for 1 hour. In a mixing bowl, stir together the broth, brown sugar, soy sauce, garlic, mustard, and onion. Stir vigorously until the sugar is completely dissolved. After an hour, remove the foil from the ribs and turn the heat up to 350°F. Carefully pour the sauce over the ribs. Re-cover with the foil and return to the oven for 1 hour. Remove the foil and bake for 15 more minutes on each side. Nutrition: Calories: 210 Total Fat: 13g Cholesterol: 70mg Sodium: 480mg Potassium: 0mg Total Carbohydrate: 3g Dietary Fiber: 0g Sugar: 0g Protein: 20g

59. Chicken BBQ Salad

Preparation time: 40 minutes Cooking Time: 15 minutes Serving: 4

Ingredients:

1 large boneless, skinless chicken breast   3 tablespoon ranch dressing   1 can of black beans   Large head of romaine lettuce   1 cup of corn kernels, fresh or frozen   3 tablespoon barbecue sauce plus more for marinating and drizzling   1 cup tri-color tortilla strips

Directions:

Place the chicken breast in a large zip-lock bag & add in the barbecue sauce; enough to cover the meat. Seal & let marinate for half an hour.   Preheat your grill over medium high heat.   Rinse the black beans, chop the romaine lettuce & heat a grill pan over medium high heat.   For dressing: Combine barbecue sauce together with ranch to taste.   Spray the grill with non-stick grilling spray & place the marinated chicken breast over the grill. Grill until the chicken is completely cooked through & juices run clear, for six minutes per side.   In the meantime, add corn to the grill pan. Lightly sprinkle with smoked paprika & grill until a few kernels are blackened slightly.   Let the chicken to rest for a few minutes and then dice into small bite-sized pieces.   Add romaine together with chicken, black beans, tortilla strips and corn in a large serving bowl. Add dressing; toss until evenly coated. Drizzle more of barbecue sauce on top of the ingredients, if desired. Serve immediately & enjoy.   Nutrition: Calories 218, Total Fat 24 g, Carbs 14 g, Protein 17 g,

60. House Salad and Dressing

Preparation Time: 10 minutes Cooking Time: 0 Servings: 12

Ingredients: Salad 1 head iceberg lettuce 1/4small red onion, sliced thin 6–12 black olives, pitted 6 pepperoncini 2 small roma tomatoes, sliced Croutons 1/4cup shredded or grated romano or parmesan cheese Dressing: 1 packet Italian dressing mix 3/4 cup vegetable/canola oil 1/4cup olive oil 1 tablespoon mayonnaise 1/3 cup white vinegar 1/4cup water 1/2teaspoon sugar 1/2teaspoon dried Italian seasoning 1/2teaspoon salt 1/4teaspoon pepper 1/4teaspoon garlic powder

Directions:

To make the dressing, combine all ingredients in a small bowl. Thoroughly whisk together. Refrigerate for 1 hour to marinate. Add the salad ingredient to a salad bowl. When ready to serve, add some of the dressing to the salad and toss to coat. Add grated cheese as a garnish as desired. Store remaining dressing in an airtight container. Keep refrigerated and it can be stored for up to 3 weeks. Nutrition: Calories 221, Total Fat 4 g, Carbs 5 g, Protein 7 g,

61. Chili's Grilled Caribbean Chicken Salad

Preparation Time: 5 minutes Cooking Time: 30 minutes Servings: 6

Ingredients: 4 boneless, skinless chicken breasts Honey-Lime Dressing 1/2cup teriyaki marinade 1/4cup Dijon mustard 1/4cup honey 1 tablespoon sesame oil 11/2teaspoons sugar 11/2cups apple cider vinegar 11/2teaspoons lime juice 2 diced tomatoes Pico De Gallo 1/2cup diced Spanish onions 2 teaspoons chopped jalapeño pepper Pinch of salt Salad 2 teaspoons minced cilantro 4 cups chopped leaf lettuce 4 handfuls of tortilla chips, broken into pieces 1 cup chopped red cabbage 4 cups chopped iceberg lettuce 1 can drained pineapple chunks

Directions: Marinate the chicken in teriyaki marinade in the refrigerator for 2 hours. Combine all the dressing ingredients in a small container, and chill in the refrigerator for 30 minutes. Mix all the pico de gallo ingredients in a small bowl, and chill in the refrigerator for 30 minutes. Preheat the grill and grill each side of the chicken breast for 5 minutes, or until done. Cut to strips. Put the lettuce and cabbage in a big salad bowl. Add the pico de gallo, dressing, pineapple and tortilla chips. Add strips of grilled chicken. Toss it in, Throw, and serve. Nutrition: Calories 218, Total Fat 8 g, Carbs 5 g, Protein 7 g,

62. Garden House Salad

Preparation Time: 5 minutes Cooking Time: 50 minutes Servings: 6

Ingredients:

1 bag of American Blend salad mix 10 black olives 10 slices red onion 8 banana peppers 1 sliced tomato 1 cup croutons Olive Garden Salad Dressing, to taste

Directions:

In a medium container with lid, mix all of the ingredients. Cool in the refrigerator for 1–2 hours with salad and serving dishes. Put the dressing onto the plate bottom. Apply the ingredients of the chilled salad over the dressing. Nutrition: Calories 245, Total Fat 6 g, Carbs 5 g, Protein 9 g,

63. Lima Beans

Preparation Time: 10 minutes Cooking time: 30 minutes Servings: 2

Ingredients:

1 cup water 1 chicken bouillon cube 2 slices bacon, chopped 1 clove garlic, peeled and lightly mashed 1/2teaspoon red pepper flakes 1/2teaspoon onion powder 1 teaspoon sugar 1/2teaspoon black pepper 1 (1-pound) bag frozen lima beans

Directions:

Add the water and bouillon cube to a large pot and bring to a boil. Stir in the remaining ingredients. Cover and turn the heat down so that the beans are simmering slightly. Allow to simmer for 30 minutes, stirring occasionally. (Add more water if necessary.) Remove the garlic and then, season with salt and pepper to taste. Nutrition: Calories 115 Protein 35 Carbs 26 Fat 5

64. Grits

Preparation Time: 10 minutes Cooking time: 30 minutes Servings: 2

Ingredients:

2 cups water 11/4cups milk 1 teaspoon salt 1 cup quick-cooking (not instant) grits 1/4cup butter

Directions:

Bring the water, milk, and salt to a boil in a small pot. Whisk the grits into the liquid, stirring constantly until they are well combined. Allow the mixture to return to a boil, then cover, reduce heat, and cook for about 30 minutes, stirring frequently. Remove from heat and stir in the butter (and cheese, if desired). Serve with butter on top. Nutrition: Calories 218, Total Fat 90 g, Carbs 66 g, Protein 39 g, Sodium 2038 mg

65. Lettuce Wraps

Preparation Time: 10 minutes Cooking Time: 10 minutes   Servings: 4

Ingredients:

1 tablespoon olive oil 2 green onions, thinly sliced   1-pound ground chicken Kosher salt and ground black pepper to taste 2 cloves garlic, minced   1 onion, diced 1/4cup hoisin sauce 1 tablespoon Sriracha (optional) 2 tablespoons soy sauce   1 tablespoon rice wine vinegar 1 tablespoon ginger, freshly grated   1 (8-ounce) can whole water chestnuts, diced and drained 1 head iceberg lettuce

Directions:

Add the oil to a deep skillet or saucepan and heat over medium-high heat. When hot, add the chicken and cook until it is completely cooked through. Stir while cooking to make sure it is properly crumbled. Drain any excess fat from the skillet, then add the garlic, onion, hoisin sauce, soy sauce, ginger, sriracha and vinegar. Cook until the onions have softened, then stir in the water chestnuts and green onion and cook for another minute or so. Add salt and pepper to taste. Serve with lettuce leaves and eat by wrapping them up like a taco. Nutrition: Calories: 157 Fat: 8 g Cholesterol: 0 mg Protein: 15.7 g Carbohydrates: 10.5 g Sugar: 2.7 g Fiber: 1.9 g

66. Clams Bruschetta

Preparation Time: 15 minutes Cooking Time: 2 minutes Servings: 8

Ingredients:

8 slices Italian bread 1 clove garlic, halved 1/2cup extra virgin olive oil 1 cup (or 2 6-ounce cans) chopped clam meat, drained 4 ripe tomatoes, cut into slices Salt and freshly ground pepper to taste 12 fresh arugula or basil leaves, rinsed and dried

Directions:

Preheat grill, then toast both sides of the bread slices. Rub the garlic onto each side of the bread to infuse with flavor. Place a tomato slice and some clam meat on each bread slice. Sprinkle with salt and pepper to taste. Drizzle olive oil on top. Cut arugula or basil thinly and place onto bruschetta. Serve. Nutrition: Calories: 424.4. Total Fat 29.4 g Cholesterol 19.3 mg Sodium 276.8 mg Total Carbohydrate 29.1 g Dietary Fiber 3.4 g Sugar: 5.2 g Protein 12.6 g

67. Brussels Sprouts N' Kale Salad

Preparation Time: 5 minutes Cooking Time: 0 minutes Servings: 6

Ingredients:

1 bunch kale 1 pound Brussels sprouts 1/4cup craisins (or dry cranberries) 1/2cup pecans, chopped Maple vinaigrette: 1/2cup olive oil 1/4cup apple cider vinegar 1/4cup maple syrup 1 teaspoon dry mustard

Directions:

Slice the kale and Brussels sprouts with a cheese grater or mandolin slicer. Transfer to a salad bowl. Add the pecans to a skillet on high heat. Toast for 60 seconds, then transfer to the salad bowl. Add the craisins. Mix all of the ingredients for the vinaigrette and whisk to combine. Pour the vinaigrette over the salad and toss. Refrigerate for a few hours or preferably overnight before serving. Nutrition: Calories 211, Total Fat 6 g, Carbs 4 g, Protein 7 g,

68. Ragù (Italian Meat Sauce)

Preparation time: 55 minutes Cooking time: 20 minutes Servings: 6

Ingredients:

For the sofrito: 2 tablespoons olive oil 1 cup chopped onion 1/2 cup chopped carrot 1/2 cup celery cut into small cubes For the ragù: 30 g dried porcini mushrooms 2 tablespoons tomato paste 5 thin slices of prosciutto 120 g minced pork 120 g ground beef 1/2 cup dry red wine 350 g of tomato puree Fine sea salt Freshly ground black pepper to taste Pinch of freshly ground nutmeg 1/2 teaspoon finely grated lemon zest

Directions:

Gather the stir-fried ingredients. Heat the olive oil in a saucepan over medium-low heat. Sauté the carrot, onion, and celery until they soften and decrease a little, and the onions are caramelized. Gather the ingredients of the ragù. Put the dried porcini mushrooms in a small bowl and cover with warm water. Let stand for 15 minutes. When the mushrooms soften, drain and store the water in a separate container. Chop the mushrooms finely and reserve. Add the tomato paste to the sauce and cook until it thickens. Add ground pork and minced meat. Increase heat to brown and stir with a wooden spoon constantly. Add the wine and mix until it evaporates. Add the chopped porcini and tomato puree. Stir and season with nutmeg, salt, and freshly ground black pepper. Pour the mushrooms soaking water and when you have finished the ragù sauce, remove it from the heat and add the sofrito and the finely grated lemon zest. Nutrition: Calories 218, Total Fat 4 g, Carbs 5 g, Protein 7 g,

69. Dave and Buster's Muffaletta Salad

Preparation Time: 5 minutes Cooking Time: 40 minutes Servings: 6

Ingredients:

24 slices pepperoni 4 ounces sliced ham 2 ounces sliced salami 4 ounces sliced turkey 1 cup roasted red peppers 1 cup sliced celery 1/4cup sliced black olives 1/4cup shredded Asiago cheese 4 tablespoons chopped green onion 1/2cup chopped green salad olives 3 tablespoons Italian dressing 11/4pounds spiral pasta 11/2cups assorted lettuce 1 cup diced Roma tomatoes 1/4cup julienned spinach leaves 1 cup Italian cheese blend

Directions:

Cut the pepperoni, salami, ham, and turkey into thin julienne pieces. Place the meats in a large bowl. Add the celery and green onions to the bowl and also the roasted peppers. Chop both types of olives into the bowl and add them to the bowl. Add the pasta after it has been cooked. Pour the Italian dressing over the pasta and gently mix everything together. Place assorted lettuce and spinach on a cold serving plate, and leave the pasta salad in the middle. Place the salad mixture up in the middle of the pot. Top the tomatoes and cheeses onto the salad. Nutrition: Calories 218, Total Fat 6 g, Carbs 8 g, Protein 7 g, Olive

BREAD AND PIZZAS

70. Meat Overload Pizza

Preparation Time: 25 minutes Cooking Time: 25 minutes Servings: 8

Ingredients

1 thin pizza crust, or crust of choice 1/2-3/4 cups marinara sauce 2 Tablespoons olive oil 1 1/2-2 pounds assorted meat like ground beef, pepperoni, Italian sausage, breakfast sausage, ham (chopped) and bacon Salt and pepper, to taste 2 cups mozzarella cheese

Directions

Heat oven to 425 degrees F. Cook bacon until crisp. Cool slightly and then crumble. Cook sausages in a little oil over medium heat to brown. Drain over paper towels. Season ground beef with salt and pepper and sauté until browned. Drain. Spread sauce over dough. Sprinkle with about 1/2 cup mozzarella followed by half of the meat ingredients. Continue layering with cheese and meat. Bake until golden brown and bubbly (about 25 minutes). Let set for 3-5 minutes before slicing. Nutrition: Calories 542 Carbs 24 g Fat 4 g Protein 32 g Sodium 1685 mg

71. Spaghetti Pizza Recipe

Preparation Time: 5 minutes Cooking Time: 30 minutes Servings: 6

Ingredients: 750 ml of pasta sauce 500 g ground beef 500 g of spaghetti 400 g of tomatoes cut into small cubes 150 g sliced pepperoni 1 1/2cups shredded cheddar cheese 1 cup shredded Swiss cheese 1/2cup grated Parmesan cheese 1/2cup whole milk 1 chopped onion 3 cloves garlic, minced 2 chopped red or green peppers 1 teaspoon dried Italian seasoning 2 large eggs

Directions: Gather the ingredients to make the spaghetti pizza. Preheat the oven to 170 ° C. Boil a large pot of water to cook the spaghetti. Cook the beef, chopped onion, chopped garlic and chopped red and green peppers in a pan over medium heat with oil until the meat is browned. Drain well and add the pasta sauce, the tomatoes cut into small cubes and the Italian seasoning. Stir well and boil over medium heat while preparing spaghetti. Cook the spaghetti according to the package instructions. Combine the milk, eggs and grated Parmesan cheese in a large bowl and beat until mixed. Strain the spaghetti and stir with the egg mixture. Spread half of the spaghetti, egg and milk mixture in a refractory dish and copper with half of the sauce and beef mixture. Repeat the layers. Bake in a preheated oven for 30 or 40 minutes until hot, and cover with the remaining cheeses and then the pepperoni. Return to the oven and bake until the cheeses melt. Let stand for five minutes and cut into squares to serve the spaghetti pizza. Nutrition: Calories 328, Total Fat 24 g, Carbs 14 g, Protein 17 g,

72. Hawaiian Pizza

Servings: 6-8 Preparation Time: 10 minutes Cooking Time: 21 minutes

Ingredients 1 pizza crust of choice 1/2 cup basic pizza sauce 2 cups shredded mozzarella cheese, divided 1/2 cup shredded Romano cheese 1 cup ham, chopped 1 cup pineapple tidbits, drained 24 slices pepperoni

Directions Preheat oven to 425 degrees. Spread sauce, beginning from the center of the crust going outward in a circular motion, leaving 1/2-inch space around the edge. Sprinkle with 1 cup mozzarella and the Romano. Arrange ham, pineapple and pepperoni slices on top and sprinkle with remaining mozzarella. Bake until cheese is melted and crust is golden brown (about 15 minutes). Nutrition: Calories 411 Carbs 46 g Fat 16 g Protein 23 g Sodium 1799 mg

73. Sausage & Mushroom

Servings: 6-8 Preparation Time: 15 minutes Cooking Time: 12 minutes

Ingredients

1 thin pizza crust dough 1/2 cup basic or marinara pizza sauce   8 ounces bulk Italian sausage, cooked and drained 1 cup fresh mushrooms, sliced thinly 1/8 teaspoon red pepper flakes, or to taste (optional)   8 ounces I shredded Italian cheese blend Parmesan cheese, grated

Directions

Preheat oven to 450 degrees F. Par-bake crust until lightly browned (about 7 minutes). Let cool slightly. Spread sauce over dough. Add sausage and mushrooms. Sprinkle with red pepper flakes (optional). Top with shredded Italian cheese blend. Bake until cheese is melted (about 5 minutes). Remove from heat and sprinkle with grated parmesan. Nutrition: Calories 348 Carbs 42 g Fat 13 g Protein 18 g Sodium 1290 mg

74. Pan Pizza Crust

Servings: 16 (2 medium size crusts) Preparation Time: 30 minutes plus 10 hours resting time Cooking Time: 12-15 minutes

Ingredients 2 1/2 cups unbleached all-purpose flour 2 teaspoons salt 1/2 teaspoon instant dry yeast   1 cup, plus 3 Tablespoons water 2 teaspoons olive oil For rectangular crust: 3 1/2 cups unbleached all-purpose flour 2 3/4 teaspoons salt 3/4 teaspoon instant dry yeast 1 2/3 cups water 3 Tablespoons olive oil

Directions Whisk flour and salt together. Whisk in yeast; Mix in water and oil until well-moistened. Cover with a towel or plastic wrap. Let rest for 8 hours. When dough is ready, grease 2 pizza pans or cast-iron skillets. Spread oil on your hands and punch dough to deflate. Divide into 2 equal portions and shape each into a ball. Oil your hands as needed. Place one portion on greased pizza pan and push down and towards the edges of the pan to shape. Repeat with other half of dough. Spread oil over the shaped dough and cover with plastic wrap. Let sit for 1 hour and then push towards sides again. Let rest another hour, at the same time preheating oven to 55 degrees F. Add desired sauce and toppings over each circle of dough. Bake until golden brown (about 12- 15 minutes). Remove from pan, if needed, and serve immediately. Nutrition: Calories 74 Carbs 4.4 g Fat 0.6 g Protein 1.9 g Sodium 291 mg

75. Breadsticks

Preparation Time: 60 minutes Cooking Time: 15 minutes Servings: 16

Ingredients: 1 1/2cups warm water 2 tablespoons sugar   Breadsticks 1/4cup butter 1 teaspoon garlic powder   1 packet (1 tablespoon/3/4 ounce) yeast 2 tablespoons butter, softened   2 teaspoons fine sea salt (and a bit extra to sprinkle on top) 4–5 cups bread flour (you can also use all-purpose flour, but the breadsticks will turn out denser)Topping

Directions:

To make the breadsticks, combine the warm water, sugar, and yeast in a large bowl. Proof for 10 minutes. Mix in the salt, softened butter, and 3 cups of bread flour. Mix in the rest of the bread flour to get a soft dough. Cover the bowl with a damp towel and set aside in a warm place. Let dough rise for 1 hour. Gently knead the dough and separate into 14–16 balls. Roll each ball into a log of your desired length. Place on two cookie sheets and let rise for 15–30 minutes. To make the topping, melt the butter and mix with the garlic powder. Brush the topping mixture over the breadsticks and finish with sprinkles of sea salt. Bake at 400°F for 12–14 minutes. Brush the remaining garlic butter on top of the breadsticks. Nutrition: Calories 190, Total Fat 4.4 g, Cholesterol 0 mg, Sodium 328 mg, Potassium 57 mg, Total Carbohydrate 31 g, Dietary fiber 1.4 g, Sugar 0.6 g, Protein 6 g

76. Creamy Mushroom with Spinach

Servings: 6-8 Preparation Time: 10 minutes Cooking Time: 22 minutes

Ingredients 1 pizza crust dough of choice 2 teaspoons cooking oil   1 cup mushrooms, sliced thinly 2 cloves garlic, minced 3 cups fresh spinach, washed and stemmed 1/2 teaspoon dried basil 1/2-3/4 cup basic white or cream white sauce 1/4 cup crumbled feta 1/2 cup mozzarella cheese, shredded

Directions Preheat oven to 425 degrees F. Par-bake crust until crust begins to brown (about 7 minutes). Remove from oven and let cool. Heat oil in a skillet over medium heat. Sauté mushrooms until tender. Add garlic and continue cooking until fragrant. Add spinach and cook until wilted. Stir in basil and remove from heat. Let cool slightly. Spread sauce over crust. Add mushroom mixture. Sprinkle with feta and mozzarella. Bake until crust is golden and cheese is melted (about 10 minutes). Nutrition: Calories 336 Carbs 36 g Fat 17 g Protein 12 g Sodium 354 mg

77. Thin Crust (with Yeast)

Serves:4-8 Preparation Time: 20 minutes Cooking Time: 8-10 minutes

Ingredients

1 teaspoon active dry yeast 1/8 cup sugar   3/4 cup lukewarm water 2 cups all-purpose flour, divided plus more for dusting 1/2 teaspoon salt

Directions

Combine yeast, sugar and water in a bowl. Whisk to dissolve yeast and let stand until mixture begins to form (about 5 minutes). Mix 1 3/4 cups of the flour and salt in a large bowl. Add in yeast mixture and mix until mixture begins to pull together. Place on a floured surface and knead lightly until smooth, adding remaining flour as needed. Roll into 1/2-inch diameter. Or, for super-thin crust, divide dough into 2 to make 2 circles. Place toppings and bake at 500 degrees F until golden (about 8-10 minutes), or follow recipe directions. Nutrition: Calories 101 Carbs 22.4 g Fat 0.0 g Protein 2.9 g Sodium 146 mg

78. Apple Pie Pizza

Servings: 6-8 Preparation Time: 20 minutes Cooking Time: 17-22 minutes

Ingredients

1 thin or pan pizza crust dough Cinnamon streusel topping: 1/2 cup packed light brown sugar 1/2 cup all-purpose flour 3/4 teaspoon cinnamon 4 tablespoons butter, softened Apple topping: 1 tablespoon butter 2 apples, peeled, cored and chopped 2 Tablespoons brown sugar 1/2 teaspoon cinnamon For glaze: 2 tablespoons butter 1/3 cup milk 1/4 teaspoon vanilla 2 cups powdered sugar

Directions

Preheat the oven to 425 degrees F. Par-bake crust just to set dough (about 5 minutes). Remove from oven and let cool. Prepare streusel topping. Combine sugar, flour and cinnamon well and the cut butter in with pastry cutter or fingers. It should have a coarse, cornmeal-like texture. Set aside. Prepare the apple mixture. Melt the butter in a skillet over medium heat. Add apples, brown sugar and cinnamon. While stirring frequently, cook until mixture begins to bubbly and fragrant (about 5 minutes). Remove from heat and let cool slightly. Spread apple mixture over crust and sprinkle with streusel topping. Bake until golden and bubbly (about 12-15 minutes). Remove from oven and let cool on a wire rack. Prepare glaze. Heat milk with butter in a saucepan over medium low to medium heat. Remove from heat as soon as butter is melted and stir in vanilla. Continue whisking while adding sugar gradually until smooth. Drizzle over apple pie pizza and serve. Nutrition: Calories 398 Carbs 87 g Fat 8 g Protein 4 g Sodium 209 mg

79. New York Style

Serves:8 Preparation Time: 15 minutes Cooking Time: 8-10 minutes

Ingredients

1 12- to 14-inch tossed pizza crust 1/2-1 cup marinara sauce 1/2 teaspoon dried oregano flakes 2 cups (8 ounces) medium dry mozzarella, shredded 2 Tablespoons parmesan,grated

Directions

Preheat oven to 500 degree F. Shred or grate all the cheeses. Spread sauce over the dough, leaving about 1/2 inch free from the edge. Sprinkle oregano flakes over sauce. Cover with shredded mozzarella, followed by grated parmesan. Bake until golden brown and bubbly (about 8-10 minutes). Let rest for cheese to set (about 3-5 minutes). Slice and serve. Nutrition: Calories 292 Carbs 22 g Fat 15 g Protein 16 g Sodium 550 mg

80. Creamy Bacon

Servings: 6-8 Preparation Time: 15 minutes Cooking Time: 15-25 minutes

Ingredients

1 pizza crust of choice 1/2-3/4 cup creamy white sauce with garlic 1 cup ricotta 6-8 strips bacon, fried crisp, drained on paper towels and chopped 1 Tablespoon bacon drippings 1/2 cup mushrooms, sliced thinly Freshly-ground black pepper, to taste Dried thyme (optional)

Directions

Preheat oven to 475 degrees F. Bake crust until lightly golden (about 10-15 minutes). Remove from oven and let cool. Heat bacon drippings in a skillet over medium heat and sauté mushrooms until tender and lightly browned (about 3-4 minutes). Remove from heat and drain on paper towels. Let cool slightly. Spread sauce and ricotta over crust. Top with mushroom and bacon. Season with black pepper and sprinkle with thyme (if using). Bake to heat through and brown crust (about 2-5 minutes). Serve immediately. Nutrition: Calories 393 Carbs 34 g Fat 22 g Protein 15 g Sodium 434 mg

81. Meat with Bell Pepper & Mushrooms

Servings: 8 Preparation Time: 15 minutes Cooking Time: 30 minutes

Ingredients

1 pizza crust of choice 1/2-3/4 cup marinara sauce 2 cups mozzarella, freshly shredded 1 1/2-2 pounds seasoned beef or pork 16-24 pieces pepperoni 1 cup mushrooms, sliced thinly 1 medium green bell pepper, sliced thinly 1 red onion, sliced Seasoned Meat Topping: 2 pounds ground lean beef or pork (or combination) 1 teaspoon ground black pepper 1 teaspoon dried parsley 1 teaspoon oregano 1 teaspoon dried basil 1/2 teaspoon garlic powder 1/2 teaspoon onion powder 1/8 teaspoon chilli flakes 1/2 teaspoon paprika 2 teaspoons salt

Directions

Preheat oven to 425 degrees F. Prepare the meat topping. Mix all the ingredients together well and sauté over medium heat until well-browned (about 10 minutes). Remove from heat and let cool. Spread sauce over crust. and sprinkle with cheese. Top with seasoned meat, pepperoni, mushrooms, bell pepper and onion. Bake until golden brown (about 20 minutes). Nutrition: Calories 496 Carbs 27 g Fat 30 g Protein 27 g Sodium 1096 mg

82. Spicy Italian Sausage Pizza

Servings: 8 Preparation Time: 10 minutes Cooking Time: 25-30 minutes

Ingredients 1 pizza crust of choice 1/2-3/4 cup basic pizza or marinara sauce 1 1/2 cups shredded mozzarella cheese 1/4 cup grated Parmigiano-Reggiano cheese 4 ounces spicy Italian turkey sausage 1 cup onion, thinly sliced 1 8-ounce package pre-sliced mushrooms 1 cup red or green bell pepper, seeded and diced (optional)

Directions Preheat oven to 450 degrees. Prepare toppings. Remove sausage from casing and cook in non stick skillet until it crumbles (about 3 minutes). Add mushrooms and onions and sauté until tender (about 4 minutes). Add bell pepper and sauté until fragrant (about 3 minutes). Remove mixture from heat and let cool. Pour pizza sauce over center of dough and spread to the sides, leaving about 1/2-inch from edge without sauce. Top with toppings. Sprinkle with mozzarella and Parmigiano-Reggiano. Bake until cheese is golden brown and bubbly (about 15-20 minutes). Nutrition: Calories 305 Carbs 45 g Fat 8 g Protein 17 g Sodium 1318 mg

83. Philly Cheesesteak Pizza

Servings: 6-8 Preparation Time: 15 minutes Cooking Time: 20-22 minutes

Ingredients

1 pizza crust of choice 1/2-3/4 cup basic or marinara sauce 2 ounces cream cheese 2 cups provolone cheese, shredded and divided 1 cup precooked roast beef, cut into thin strips 1/3 cup pickled pepper rings 1/4 cup grated Parmesan cheese 1/2 teaspoon dried oregano For pepper mixture: 1 Tablespoon olive oil 2 small bell peppers (green, red or combination), sliced into thin strips 1 1/2 cups sliced fresh mushrooms 1 small onion, chopped

Directions

Preheat oven to 450 degrees F. Par bake crust until set (about 5 minutes). Remove from oven and let cool. Prepare pepper mixture. Heat oil in a skillet over medium heat and add peppers, mushrooms and onion. Sauté until tender. Remove from heat and let cool. Spread sauce over crust. Scoop cream cheese evenly on top and sprinkle with 1 cup provolone. Add beef, pepper mixture and pepper rings. Sprinkle with remaining provolone, parmesan and oregano. Bake until crust is golden and cheese is melted (about 10-12 minutes). Nutrition: Calories 439 Carbs 36 g Fat 20 g Protein 29 g Sodium 826 mg

84. Sicilian Pizza

Servings: 8-12 Preparation Time: 15 minutes Cooking Time: 10 minutes

Ingredients

1 rectangular pan pizza crust   1/2 cup marinara sauce 1 pound mozzarella cheese, sliced thinly 12 ounces pepperoni, sliced thinly 4 ounces ground Pecorino Romano cheese, divided Fresh basil leaves (optional)

Directions

Preheat oven to 550 degrees F. Arrange the mozzarella slices so that dough is covered evenly. Spread marinara sauce over cheese. Cover with pepperoni slices and sprinkle with half of the ground cheese. Bake until crust is browned and pepperoni look crisp (about 10 minutes). Lift slightly to check bottom of crust (It should be golden brown). Sprinkle with remaining cheese and serve immediately. Nutrition: Calories 337 Carbs 6 g Fat 24 g Protein 18 g Sodium 1177 mg

85. Taco Bell's The Mexican Pizza

Preparation Time: 30 minutes Cooking Time: 12 minutes Servings: 4

Ingredients

1/2pound ground beef 1/2teaspoon salt 1/4teaspoon onion, finely chopped 1/4teaspoon paprika 11/2teaspoon chili powder 2 tablespoons water 1 cup vegetable oil 8 6-inch flour tortillas 1 16-ounce can refried beans 2/3 cup Picante sauce 1/3 cup tomato, finely chopped 1 cup cheddar cheese, grated 1 cup Colby Jack cheese, grated 1/4cup green onion, diced 1/4cup black olives, chopped

Directions

Preheat oven to 400°F. In a skillet, sauté beef on medium heat. Once brown, drain. Then stir in salt, onions, paprika, chili powder, and water. While continuously stirring, cook for an additional 10 minutes. In a separate skillet add oil and heat over medium-high. Cook tortilla for about 30 seconds on both sides or until golden brown. Use a fork to pierce any bubbles forming on the tortillas. Transfer onto a plate lined with paper towels. Microwave refried beans on high for about 30 seconds or until warm. To build each pizza, coat 1/3 cup beans on tortilla followed by 1/3 cup cooked beef. Top with a second tortilla. Cover with 2 tablespoons Picante sauce, then equal amounts of tomatoes, cheeses, green onions, and olives. This makes a total of 4 pizzas. Place prepared pizzas on a baking sheet. Bake in the oven until cheese is fully melted, about 8 to 12 minutes. Serve. Nutrition: Calories 245 Carbs 2 g Fat 8.2 g Protein 12 g

86. Veggie Pizza

Servings: 6-8 Preparation Time: 15 minutes Cooking Time: 20 minutes

Ingredients 1 thin pizza crust dough, or dough of choice 1/2 cup marinara sauce 3 roma tomatoes, sliced 1 cup mushrooms, sliced thinly 1 red onion, sliced thinly 1 large green bell pepper, seeded and sliced into strips 1/4 cup black olives, pitted and sliced 2 cups mozzarella cheese, shredded

Directions Preheat oven to 450 degrees F. Spreads sauce over crust dough. Arrange the tomatoes, mushrooms, onion, pepper and olives on top as desired. Sprinkle with shredded mozzarella. Bake until golden and bubbly (about 20 minutes). Let set for 3 minutes before slicing. Nutrition: Calories 227 Carbs 27g Fat 9 g Protein 10 g Sodium 235 mg

87. Tomato Pie

Servings: 8-12 Preparation Time: 5 minutes Cooking Time: 25-30 minutes

Ingredients

1 rectangular pan pizza dough 2 Tablespoons unsalted butter 1 small onion, minced 1 Tablespoon sugar 1 1/2 cups marinara sauce 2 Tablespoons Pecorino Romano cheese, finely grated

Directions

Preheat oven to 450 degrees F. Par-bake crust until very lightly browned (about 10 minutes). Remove from oven and let cool slightly. In a skillet or saucepan, combine butter and onion. Cook over medium low heat, until onion is tender (about 3-5 minutes). Remove from heat. Add marinara sauce and sugar. Stir until sugar is dissolved. Spread enough sauce to cover the crust generously. Bake until crust is golden brown (about 15-20 minutes). Sprinkle with parmesan and serve warm. Nutrition: Calories 216 Carbs 29 g Fat 9 g Protein 4 g Sodium 413 mg

88. Thin Crust (Yeast-Free)

Servings: 4-8 Preparation Time: 20 minutes plus 10 minutes resting time Cooking Time: 20-23 minutes (with par-baking)

Ingredients

1 1/3 cups all-purpose flour 1 teaspoon baking powder 1/2 teaspoon salt 1/2 cup fat-free milk 2 Tablespoons olive oil

Directions

Whisk dry ingredients together. Mix while adding milk and olive oil until the mixture begins to stick together. Transfer to a floured surface and knead until smooth. Shape into a ball, cover and let rest for 10 minutes. Roll out into a 12-inch circle. Transfer to a lined baking sheet and bake in a preheated oven at 400 degrees F to just to set (about 5-8 minutes). Add toppings and return to oven. Bake until golden brown (about 15 minutes). Nutrition: Calories 112 Carbs 16.9 g Fat 3.6 g Protein 2.8 g Sodium 216 mg

89. Deep Dish

Serves:8 Preparation Time: 20 minutes plus 4-6 hours resting time Cooking Time: 5 minutes

Ingredients

1 1/2 teaspoons active dry yeast   1 Tablespoon sugar or honey 3/4 cup lukewarm water 1 1/2 cups all-purpose flour, plus more for dusting 1/2 cup semolina flour (optional; if not using, add 1/2 cup all-purpose flour) 1/2 teaspoon salt 1/8 teaspoon cream of tartar 2/3 corn oil plus more for greasing 2 Tablespoons butter, softened (optional)

Directions

In a small bowl, dissolve yeast and sugar in lukewarm water. Let sit for 15 minutes. In a large bowl, whisk flour(s), salt and cream of tartar together. Make a well and pour in the yeast mixture and oil. Using a mixer with hook attachment, mix briefly to moisten (about 1 minutes) Knead for a short while (2 minutes) to get a shortbread-type texture when baked.   Cover with a towel or cling wrap and let rise for 4-6 hours. You may need to oil the dough to avoid crusting, depending on the humidity in your area. Preheat oven to 450 degrees F. Grease pan (You may use a 9 1/2-inch deep-dish pie pan, springform pan or 10-inch cast iron pan). Punch down dough, cover and let rest (15 minutes). Roll out and place in greased pan or press down with hands over pan (Dough will be sticky; dust with flour for easier handling).   Bake just until set and matte in appearance (about 5 minutes). Brush dough with butter, if using. Add desired toppings and sauce and bake until golden brown (about 35-40 minutes). Nutrition: Calories 282 Carbs 25.7 g Fat 18.4 g Protein 3.9 g Sodium 148 mg

90. Steamed White Clam Pizza

Servings: 2-4 Preparation Time: 2 hours 15 minutes Cooking Time: 10-12 minutes

Ingredients

1 thin crust pizza dough 3/4 cup chopped clams, drained well   4 garlic cloves, minced 1 Tablespoon dried oregano   1/2 cup extra virgin olive oil 3/4 cup Pecorino Romano cheese, grated

Directions

Preheat the oven to 400°F. Gently mix together drained clams, olive oil, garlic and oregano. Spread evenly over crust. Sprinkle with cheese.   Bake until golden brown (about 10–15 minutes). Nutrition: Calories 300 Carbs 8 g Fat 12 g Protein 45 g Sodium 300mg

POULTRY AND FISH RECIPES

91. Chicken Fried Chicken

Preparation Time: 10 minutes Cooking time: 30 minutes Servings: 4

Ingredients:

Chicken 1/2cup all-purpose flour 1 teaspoon poultry seasoning 1/2teaspoon salt 1/2teaspoon pepper 1 egg, slightly beaten 1 tablespoon water 4 boneless skinless chicken breasts, pounded to a ½-inch thickness 1 cup vegetable oil Gravy 2 tablespoons all-purpose flour 1/4teaspoon salt 1/4teaspoon pepper 11/4cups milk

Directions:

Preheat the oven to 200°F. In a shallow dish, combine the flour, poultry seasoning, salt, and pepper. In another shallow dish, mix the beaten egg and water. First, dip both sides of the chicken breasts in the flour mixture, then dip them in the egg mixture, and then back into the flour mixture. Heat the vegetable oil over medium-high heat in a large deep skillet. A cast iron is a good choice if you have one. Add the chicken and cook for about 15 minutes, or until fully cooked, turning over about halfway through. Transfer the chicken to a cookie sheet and place in the oven to maintain temperature. Remove all but 2 tablespoons of oil from the skillet you cooked the chicken in. Prepare the gravy by whisking the dry gravy ingredients together in a bowl. Then whisk them into the oil in the skillet, stirring thoroughly to remove lumps. When the flour begins to brown, slowly whisk in the milk. Continue cooking and whisking for about 2 minutes or until the mixture thickens. Top chicken with some of the gravy. Nutrition: Calories: 281 Total Fat: 30g Carbs: 32g Protein: 71g Fiber: 0g

92. Chicken Casserole

Preparation Time: 10 minutes Cooking time: 60 minutes Servings: 4

Ingredients:

Crust 1 cup yellow cornmeal 1/3 cup all-purpose flour 11/2teaspoons baking powder 1 tablespoon sugar 1/2teaspoon salt 1/2teaspoon baking soda 2 tablespoons vegetable oil 3/4 cup buttermilk 1 egg Filling 21/2cups cooked chicken breast, cut into bite-sized pieces 1/4cup chopped yellow onion 1/2cup sliced celery 1 teaspoon salt 1/4teaspoon ground pepper 1 (10.5-ounce) can condensed cream of chicken soup 13/4 cups chicken broth 2 tablespoons butter 1/2cup melted butter

Directions:

Preheat the oven to 375°F. To make the crust, in a large bowl, combine all of the crust ingredients until smooth. Dump this mixture into a buttered or greased 8 by 8-inch baking dish. Bake for about 20 minutes, then remove from oven and allow to cool. Reduce oven temperature to 350°F. Crumble the cooled cornbread mixture. Add to a large mixing bowl along with 1/2cup of melted butter. Set aside. Make the chicken filling by adding the butter to a large saucepan over medium heat. Let it melt, then add the celery and onions and cook until soft. Add the chicken broth, cream of chicken soup, salt, and pepper. Stir until everything is well combined. Add the cooked chicken breast pieces and stir again. Cook for 5 minutes at a low simmer. Transfer the filling mixture into 4 individual greased baking dishes or a greased casserole dish. Top with the cornbread mixture and transfer to the oven. Bake for 35–40 minutes for a large casserole dish or 25–30 minutes for individual dishes. Nutrition: Calories: 381 Total Fat: 30g Carbs: 32g Protein: 71g Fiber: 0g

93. Chicken Pot Pie

Preparation Time: 30 minutes Cooking time: 45 minutes Servings: 4

Ingredients:

1/2cup butter 1 medium onion, diced 1 (14.5-ounce) can chicken broth 1 cup half and half milk 1/2cup all-purpose flour 1 carrot, diced 1 celery stalk, diced 3 medium potatoes, peeled and diced 3 cups cooked chicken, diced 1/2cup frozen peas 1 teaspoon chicken seasoning 1/2teaspoon salt 1/2teaspoon ground pepper 1 single refrigerated pie crust 1 egg Water

Directions:

Preheat the oven to 375°F. In a large skillet, heat the butter over medium heat, add the leeks and sauté for 3 minutes. Sprinkle flour over the mixture, and continue to stir constantly for 3 minutes. Whisking constantly, blend in the chicken broth and milk. Bring the mixture to a boil. Reduce heat to medium-low. Add the carrots, celery, potatoes, salt, pepper, and stir to combine. Cook for 10-15 minutes or until veggies are cooked through but still crisp. Add chicken and peas. Stir to combine. Transfer chicken filling to a deep 9-inch pie dish.   Fit the pie crust sheet on top and press the edges around the dish to seal the crust. Trim the excess if needed. In a separate bowl, whisk an egg with 1 tablespoon of water, and brush the mixture over the top of the pie. With a knife, cut a few slits to let steam escape.   Bake the pie in the oven on the middle oven rack 20 to 30 minutes until the crust becomes golden brown. Let the pie rest for about 15 minutes before serving. Note: Alternatively to serve it like exactly Cracker Barrel, use individual baking dishes and proceed the same way, using homemade or store-bought crust that you can roll out will make it easier to shape the required crust for each dish. Nutrition: Calories: 111 Total Fat: 23g Carbs: 12g Protein: 81g Fiber: 0g

94. Farm-Raised Catfish

Preparation Time: 10 minutes Cooking time: 45 minutes Servings: 4

Ingredients:

1/4cup all-purpose flour 1/4cup cornmeal 1 teaspoon onion powder 1 teaspoon dried basil 1/2teaspoon garlic salt 1/2teaspoon dried thyme 1/4–1/2teaspoon white pepper 1/4–1/2teaspoon cayenne pepper 1/4–1/2teaspoon black pepper 4 catfish fillets (6–8 ounces each) 1/4cup butter

Directions:

Add the flour, cornmeal, onion powder, basil, salt, thyme, white pepper, cayenne pepper, and black pepper to a large plastic freezer bag. Place the catfish fillets in the bag and gently shake to coat. Fish breaks easily, so be careful! Heat a large skillet over medium-high heat. Add the butter, and when it melts, lay in the catfish. Cook, covered, for 8–10 minutes on each side, or until the fish flakes easily with a fork. Nutrition: Calories: 112 Total Fat: 23g Carbs: 12g Protein: 81g Fiber: 0g

95. Honey Grilled Salmon

Preparation Time: 10 minutes Cooking time 30 minutes Servings 4

Ingredients

1/4cup of honey 1/3 cup of soy sauce 1/4cup of dark brown sugar, packed 1/4cup of pineapple juice 2 tablespoons fresh lemon juice 1 tablespoon apple cider vinegar 1 tablespoon olive oil 1 teaspoon ground black pepper, plus more for seasoning the salmon 1/2teaspoon cayenne pepper 1/2teaspoon paprika 1/2teaspoon garlic powder 4 (8 ounces) salmon fillets Rice and vegetables, to serve

Directions

In a medium saucepan over medium-low heat, combine all the ingredients except the fish. Bring it to a boil, then reduce the warmth, occasionally stirring until the sauce thickens to the consistency of syrup. Cook the salmon to your preference, either on the grill or in the oven. Serve the salmon with sauce over the highest, with rice and vegetables. Nutrition: Calories: 233 Total Fat: 14g Carbs: 36g Protein: 44g Fiber:0g

96. Chang's Kung Pao Shrimp

Preparation Time: 10 minutes Cooking time 10 minutes Servings 4

Ingredients

1/4cup of soy sauce 1/2teaspoon of cornstarch 2 tablespoons of water 1/4teaspoon of sesame oil 1/2teaspoon of balsamic vinegar 1/2teaspoon of sugar Pepper to taste 3 tablespoons of hot chili oil 3 cloves of garlic, minced 1/4onion, roughly chopped 16 large shrimp, peeled and deveined 1/4cup of roasted peanuts 5 scallions, chopped

Directions

In a bowl, whisk together the soy, cornstarch, water, vegetable oil, balsamic vinegar, sugar, and pepper. Set aside. Add the recent chili oil to a deep skillet or wok and warmth over medium-high heat. Add the minced garlic and onion and cook for about 2 minutes. If you would like to feature other vegetables, like broccoli or peas, you'll add them now. Cook until the veggies are soft. Add the shrimp and cook for about 2 minutes, then stir in the sauce you made earlier and cooked a touch longer until the sauce thickens. Stir to coat the shrimp, remove the skillet from the warmth and stir in the scallions and peanuts. Serve with rice. Nutrition: Calories: 760 Total Fat: 52g Carbs: 39g Protein: 40g Fiber:15g

97. Orange Chicken

Preparation Time: 15 minutes Cooking Time: 30 minutes Servings: 6

Ingredients:

Orange sauce: 11/2tablespoon soy sauce   11/2tablespoon water   5 tablespoons sugar   5 tablespoons white vinegar   3 tablespoons orange zest   Chicken preparation: 1 egg   11/2teaspoon salt   White pepper, to taste   5 tablespoons grapeseed oil, divided   1/2cup + 1 tablespoon cornstarch   1/4cup flour   1/4cup cold water   2 pounds chicken breast, boneless and skinless, chopped   1 teaspoon fresh ginger, grated   1 teaspoon garlic, finely chopped   1/2teaspoon hot red chili pepper, ground   1/4cup green onion, sliced   1 tablespoon rice wine   1/2teaspoon sesame oil   White rice and steamed broccoli for serving

Directions:

Mix together Ingredients: for the orange sauce in a bowl. Reserve for future. Add egg, salt, pepper, and 1 tablespoon oil to a separate bowl. Mix well. In another bowl, combine 1/2cup cornstarch and flour. Mix until fully blended. Add remaining cornstarch and cold water in a different bowl. Blend until cornstarch is completely dissolved. Heat 3 tablespoons oil in a large deep skillet or wok over high heat. Coat chicken pieces in egg mixture. Let excess drip off. Then, coat in cornstarch mixture. Cook for at least 3 minutes or until both sides are golden brown and chicken is cooked through. Arrange on a plate lined with paper towels to drain excess oil. In a clean large deep skillet, or wok heat remaining oil on high heat. Lightly sauté ginger and garlic for 30 seconds or until aromatic. Toss in peppers and green onions. Stir-fry vegetables for 1-3 minutes, then pour in rice wine. Mix well before adding orange sauce. Bring to a boil. Mix in cooked chicken pieces, then add cornstarch mixture. Simmer until mixture is thick, then mix in sesame oil. Nutrition: Calories: 305 Fat: 5 g Carbs: 27 g Protein: 34 g Sodium: 1024 mg

98. Chicken and Dumplings

Preparation Time: 1 hour Cooking Time: 2 hours Servings: 6

Ingredients:

1 whole chicken 2 quarts water 2 teaspoons salt 1/2teaspoon pepper 2 cups all-purpose flour 1/2teaspoon baking soda 1/2teaspoon salt 3 tablespoons shortening 3/4 cup buttermilk

Directions:

In a heavy bottomed pot, boil chicken in water mixed with salt. Cover, then lower heat. Simmer for about 1 hour or until tender enough that the meat almost falls off the bone. Using a slotted spoon, transfer chicken to a plate and cool. Then, remove bones and chop into small pieces. In same pot, add broth and bring to a boil Add pepper. In a bowl, mix flour, baking soda, and salt. Fold in shortening. Pour in buttermilk and mix everything until incorporated. Knead dough 4 to 5 times. Pinch off about 1/2inch size balls of dough and to the boiling broth. Reduce heat to medium-low. Simmer for about 8 to 10 minutes while stirring every now and then. Add chicken to pot and stir. Serve immediately. Nutrition: Calories: 711 Fat: 41 g Saturated fat: 12 g Carbs: 33 g Sugar: 2 g Fibers: 1 g Protein: 48 g Sodium: 1276 mg

99. Broccoli Cheddar Chicken

Preparation Time: 10 minutes Cooking time: 45 minutes Servings: 4

Ingredients:

4 skinless chicken breasts 1 cup milk 1 cup Ritz-style crackers, crushed 1 (10.5-ounce) can condensed cheddar cheese soup 1/2pound frozen broccoli 6 ounces cheddar cheese, shredded 1/2teaspoon salt 1/2teaspoon pepper

Directions:

Preheat the oven to 350°F. Whisk the milk and cheddar cheese soup together in a mixing bowl. Prepare a baking dish by greasing the sides, then lay the chicken in the bottom and season with the salt and pepper. Pour the soup mixture over the chicken, then top with the crackers, broccoli, and shredded cheese. Bake for about 45 minutes or until bubbly. Nutrition: Calories: 181 Total Fat: 30g Carbs: 32g Protein: 71g Fiber: 0g

100.   Creamy Chicken and Rice

Preparation Time: 10 minutes Cooking time: 45 minutes Servings: 4

Ingredients:

Salt and pepper to taste 2 cups cooked rice 1 diced onion 1 can cream of mushroom soup 1 packet chicken gravy 11/2pounds chicken breasts, cut into strips

Directions:

Preheat the oven to 350°F. Cook the rice. When it is just about finished, toss in the diced onion so that it cooks too. Prepare a baking dish by greasing or spraying with nonstick cooking spray. Dump the rice into the prepared baking dish. Layer the chicken strips on top. Spread the undiluted cream of mushroom soup over the chicken. In a small bowl, whisk together the chicken gravy with 1 cup of water, making sure to get all the lumps out. Pour this over the top of the casserole. Cover with foil and transfer to the oven. Bake for 45 minutes or until the chicken is completely cooked. Nutrition: Calories: 111 Total Fat: 23g Carbs: 12g Protein: 81g Fiber: 0g

101.   Cornflake Crusted Chicken

Preparation Time: 10 minutes Cooking time: 45 minutes Servings: 4

Ingredients:

4 boneless skinless chicken breasts, cut into large strips 3 cups cornflakes 2 tablespoons melted butter 1 large egg, beaten 1 teaspoon water Salt Pepper Chicken poultry seasoning

Directions:

Preheat the oven to 400°F. Lay out the chicken breasts and season both sides with salt, pepper, and poultry seasoning. In a shallow dish, combine the water and egg. In a separate shallow dish, crush the cornflakes and season with some more poultry seasoning. Dip each breast in the egg mixture, then roll it in the cornflakes. Place the chicken on a baking sheet and pat more cornflakes on top. Bake for about 30–35 minutes or until the chicken is done. Nutrition: Calories: 121 Total Fat: 23g Carbs: 12g Protein: 81g Fiber: 0g

102. Bonefish Grill's Bang-Bang Shrimp

Preparation Time: 5 minutes Cooking Time: 5 minutes Servings: 4

Ingredients

1/2cup of mayonnaise 1/4cup of Thai sweet chili sauce 3-5 drops of hot chili sauce (or more if you like it spicier) 1/2cup of cornstarch 1-pound of small shrimp, peeled and deveined 11/2cups of vegetable oil

Directions

To make the sauce, combine mayonnaise with Thai condiment and hot condiment in a bowl. In a separate bowl, add cornstarch. Toss shrimp in cornstarch until well-coated. Heat oil in a wok. Work in batches, fry shrimp until golden brown, about 2-3 minutes. Transfer onto a plate lined with paper towels to empty excess oil. Serve shrimp in a bowl with sauce drizzled on top. Nutrition: Calories 274, Total Fat 11 g, Carbs 26 g, Protein 16 g, Sodium 1086 mg

103. Apple Cheddar Chicken

Preparation Time: 10 minutes Cooking time: 45 minutes Servings: 4

Ingredients:

5 cooked skinless chicken breasts, whole or cubed (Cracker Barrel uses the whole breast, but either option works just as well.) 2 cans apple pie filling, cut apples in third 1 bag extra-sharp cheddar cheese 1 row Ritz crackers, crushed 1 cup melted butter

Directions:

Preheat the oven to 350°F. Combine the chicken, apple pie filling, and cheddar cheese in a mixing bowl. Stir to combine. Pour the mixture into a greased casserole dish. Mix Ritz crackers with the melted butter. Spread over the casserole. Bake for 45 minutes or until it starts to bubble. Nutrition: Calories: 111 Total Fat: 23g Carbs: 12g Protein: 81g Fiber: 0g

104. Teriyaki Filet Medallions

Preparation Time: 15 minutes Cooking time: 20 minutes Servings: 4

Ingredients:

3 (6-ounce) sirloin or ribeye steaks 1 red bell pepper, cut in 1-inch squares 1 yellow bell pepper, cut in 1-inch squares 1 green pepper, cut in 1-inch squares 1 large red onion, outer layers cut in 1-inch squares Teriyaki marinade 1 cup soy sauce 1/2cup Apple Cider Vinegar 1/2cup Sugar 1/2cup Pineapple Juice 2 cloves garlic, minced 2 teaspoons fresh ginger, grated 1 teaspoon red pepper flakes

Directions:

In a mixing bowl, combine the marinade ingredients. Cut the steaks in 1-inch cubes and place them in a resalable bag. Reserve a third of the marinade and pour the rest over the meat. Seal and refrigerate for 4 hours or more, manipulating the bag from time to time. Soak your skewers if they're wooden and heat the grill to medium. Thread the skewers by alternating meat and vegetables. Grill for 5–10 minutes on each side, brushing often with the reserved marinade. Nutrition: Calories: 681 Total Fat: 30g Carbs: 32g Protein: 71g Fiber: 0g Protein: 59 g Sodium: 1043 mg

105.   Fried Chicken

Preparation Time: 20 minutes Cooking Time: 40 minutes Servings: 4

Ingredients:

Spice mix: 1 tablespoon paprika   2 teaspoons onion salt   1 teaspoon chili powder   1 teaspoon black pepper, ground   1/2teaspoon celery salt   1/2teaspoon dried sage   1/2teaspoon garlic powder   1/2teaspoon allspice, ground   1/2teaspoon dried oregano   1/2teaspoon dried basil   1/2teaspoon dried marjoram   Chicken preparation: 1 whole chicken, cut into parts 2 quarts frying oil   1 egg white   1 1/2cups all-purpose flour   1 tablespoon brown sugar   1 tablespoon kosher salt

Directions:

Preheat oil in deep fryer to 350°F.   In a bowl, mix together Ingredients: for the spice mix. Then, add flour, sugar, and salt. Mix well until fully blended.   Coat each chicken piece with egg white, then the flour breading. Make sure that the chicken pieces are well-coated.   Transfer to a plate and allow chicken to dry for about 5 minutes.   Deep-fry breasts and wings together for about 12 minutes or until the temperature on a meat thermometer inserted in the breast's thickest part reads 165 °F. Do the same with legs and thighs. Usually these parts take 1-2 minutes more to cook.   Transfer pieces onto a plate lined with paper towels.   Serve.
Nutrition: Calories: 418 Fat: 22 g Carbs: 41 g Protein: 15 g Sodium: 1495 mg

BEEF AND PORK RECIPES

106. **DIY Sizzling Steak, Cheese, and Mushrooms Skillet**

Preparation Time: 15 minutes Cooking Time: 1 hour 35 minutes Servings: 4

Ingredients:

1 head garlic, cut crosswise   2 tablespoons olive oil, divided   Salt and pepper, to taste   2 pounds Yukon Gold potatoes, chopped into 1-inch pieces   Water, for boiling   2 tablespoons butter   1 large yellow onion   8 ounces cremini mushrooms   Salt and pepper to taste   1/2cup milk   1/4cup cream   3 tablespoons butter   21/2pounds 1-inch thick sirloin steak, cut into 4 large pieces   8 slices mozzarella cheese

Directions:

Preheat oven to 300°F.   Position garlic on foil. Pour 1 tablespoon olive oil to the inner sides where the garlic was cut, then wrap foil around garlic.   Place in oven and bake for 30 minutes. Remove from oven and squeeze out garlic from head. Transfer to a bowl or mortar. Add salt and pepper, then mash together. Set aside.   In a pot, add potatoes. Pour enough water on top to cover potatoes. Bring to a boil. Once boiling, reduce heat to medium. Simmer for about 20 to 25 minutes or until potatoes become tender.   Melt butter on a non-stick pan over medium-low heat. Add onions and sauté for about 15 minutes until a bit tender. Toss in mushrooms and sauté, adjusting heat to medium. Season with salt and pepper. Cook for 10 minutes more. Set aside and keep warm.   Drain potatoes, then mash using an electric mixer on low speed. While mashing, gradually pour in milk, cream, butter, and mashed garlic with olive oil. Keep blending until everything is cream-like and smooth. Remove from mixer and place a cover on top of bowl. Set aside and keep warm.   Evenly coat steak pieces with remaining 1 tablespoon olive oil on all sides. Heat grill, then place meat on grill. Cook for 4 minutes. Flip and add mozzarella slices on top. Cook for another 4 minutes for medium rare. Add additional minutes for increased doneness.   Transfer steaks to serving plates then top with onion/mushroom mixture. Place mashed potatoes on the side. Serve.   Nutrition: Calories: 270 Total Fat: 0g Carbs: 0g Protein: 22g Fiber: 0g

107. Quesadilla Burger

Preparation time: 15 minutes Cooking time: 15 minutes Servings: 4

Ingredients:

1 1/2pounds ground beef 8 (6-inch) flour tortillas 1 tablespoon butter   Tex-Mex seasoning for the burgers   2 teaspoons ground cumin 2 tablespoons paprika 1 teaspoon black pepper   1/2teaspoon cayenne pepper, more or less depending on taste   1 teaspoon salt or to taste 1 tablespoon dried oregano   Toppings 8 slices pepper jack cheese 4 slices Applewood-smoked bacon, cooked and crumbled   1/2cup shredded iceberg lettuce   Pico de Galo   1-2 Roma tomatoes, deseeded and diced thin   ½-1 tablespoon thinly diced onion (red or yellow is fine) 1-2 teaspoons fresh lime juice   1-2 teaspoons fresh cilantro, chopped finely   1-2 teaspoons thinly diced jalapeños pepper - Salt and pepper to taste   Tex-Mex ranch dressing 1/2cup sour cream 1/2cup ranch dressing such as Hidden Valley   1 teaspoon Tex-Mex seasoning 1/4cup mild salsa   Pepper to taste - For serving (optional) - Guacamole, and sour cream

Directions:

In a mixing bowl, combine the Tex-Mex seasoning ingredients and stir to ensure they are well combined.   Prepare the fresh Pico de Gallo by mixing all the ingredients in a bowl. Set aside in the refrigerator until ready to use.   Prepare the Tex-Mex ranch dressing by mixing all the ingredients in a bowl. Set aside in the refrigerator until ready to use.   Add 2 tablespoons of the Tex-Mex seasoning to the ground beef and mix it in, being careful not to overwork the beef or your burgers will be tough. Form into 4 large ¼-inch thick burger patties and cook either on the grill or in a skillet to your preference.   Heat a clean skillet over medium-low heat. Butter each of the flour tortillas on one side. Place one butter side down in the skillet. Top with 1 slice of cheese, some shredded lettuce, some Pico de Gallo, some bacon, and then top with a cooked burger. Top the burger with some of the Tex-Mex ranch dressing sauce to taste, some Pico the Gallo, bacon, and another slice of cheese.   Cover with another tortilla, butter side up. Cook for about 1 minute or until the tortilla is golden. Then carefully flip the tortilla and cook until the cheese has melted. This step can be done in a sandwich press if you have one.   Cut the tortillas in quarters or halves and serve with a side of the Tex-Mex ranch dressing, guacamole, and sour cream, if desired.   Nutrition: Calories: 1330, Total Fat: 93 g, Cholesterol: 240 mg, Sodium: 3000 mg, Total Carbohydrate: 50 g, Dietary Fiber: 6 g, Sugars: 7 g, Protein: 74 g

108. Texas Roadhouse's Red Chili

Preparation time: 20 minutes Cooking time: 1 hour Servings: 6

Ingredients

2 tablespoons vegetable oil 2 pounds beef chuck, cut into bite-sized cubes 1 yellow onion, diced 2 cloves garlic, chopped 1 1/2teaspoons chili powder 1 teaspoon ground cumin 1 teaspoon paprika 1 teaspoon salt 1/2teaspoon black pepper 1/4teaspoon red pepper flakes 1 tablespoon brown sugar 1 1/2cups crushed tomatoes 2 teaspoons white vinegar 1 (15-ounce) can red kidney beans 2 jalapeños, seeded and sliced   Optional for topping Shredded cheddar   Green onions, chopped

Directions

In a large pot or Dutch oven, heat the oil and brown the meat well on all sides. Add the onion and cook to soften, and then stir in the garlic and cook until fragrant. Add the chili powder, cumin, paprika, salt, pepper, red pepper flakes, and brown sugar. Mix to combine. Stir in the crushed tomatoes and vinegar. Bring the pot to a simmer, cover, and cook for 30 minutes. Add the kidney beans and jalapeños and cook 10 more minutes.   Serve hot with a sprinkle of shredded cheese and green onion.
Nutrition: Calories 201 Carbs 2 g Fat 8.2 g Protein 9.3 g

109.   Café Rio's Sweet Pork Salad

Preparation time: 20 minutes Cooking time: 5 hours Servings: 12

Ingredients

For the Meat 6 pounds pork shoulder (yields about 4 pounds cooked, fat removed, shredded pork) 1 1/2teaspoons onion salt 1/2teaspoon ground black pepper 2 cloves garlic, crushed and minced 1 can cola (not diet) For the Sauce 2 (4-ounce) cans diced mild to medium green chilies 1 1/2cups red enchilada sauce 1 cup brown sugar 2 cloves garlic, chopped 1 can cola   For the Filling Guacamole Café Rio Black Beans Cilantro Lime Rice For Serving (optional) 6 corn tortillas, sliced into strips and fried 12–16 flour tortillas, softened (or 1 per serving), warmed Lettuce, chopped Tomatoes, sliced Sweet onion, sliced Cheddar or Mexican blend cheese, shredded Pico de Gallo or salsa Sour cream Cilantro, chopped

Directions

Preheat the oven to 350°F and place the rack in the bottom third (or use a slow cooker). Season the roast with onion salt and black pepper. Rub the garlic on the top of the meat. Place the roast in the roasting pan (or slow cooker) and pour the cola at the bottom. Cover tightly and roast for 2 hours without opening the oven. Reduce the heat to 200°F and bake 3 more hours. (If using a slow cooker, cook on LOW for 5 hours.) Meanwhile, prepare the black beans and cilantro rice.   Remove the meat from the pot and let it cool for about 20 minutes. Remove any visible fat and shred the meat. Drain the pan and place the meat back in it. Prepare the sauce. Place the chilies, enchilada sauce, garlic, and brown sugar in a blender and mix. Add the cola and stir it in with a spoon. Pour the sauce over the meat and jiggle the pan to coat the meat. Place it back in the oven to heat through. To assemble the salad, place a warm flour tortilla on a plate and layer on beans, rice, meat, lettuce, tomato, onion, cheese, guacamole, pico de gallo, sour cream, and cilantro. Nutrition: Calories 265 Carbs 2 g Fat 8.2 g Protein 11 g

110.   Meat Loaf

Preparation Time: 15 minutes Cooking Time: 1 1/2hours Servings: 6

Ingredients:

2 large eggs 2/3 cup whole milk 3 slices bread, torn 1/2 cup chopped onion 1/2 cup grated carrot 1 cup shredded cheddar or part-skim mozzarella cheese 1 tablespoon minced fresh parsley or 1 teaspoon dried parsley 1 teaspoon dried basil, thyme, or sage, optional 1 teaspoon salt 1/4 teaspoon pepper 1-1/2 pounds lean ground beef TOPPING: 1/2 cup tomato sauce 1/2 cup packed brown sugar 1 teaspoon prepared mustard

Directions

In a large bowl, beat eggs. Add milk and bread; let stand until liquid is absorbed. Stir in the onion, carrot, cheese, and seasonings. Crumble beef over mixture and mix well. Shape into a 7-1/2x3-1/2x2-1/2-in. loaf in a shallow baking pan. Bake, uncovered, at 350° for 45 minutes. Combine the topping ingredients, spoon half of the mixture over meat loaf. Bake 30 minutes longer or until meat is no longer pink and a thermometer reads 160°, occasionally spooning remaining topping over loaf. Let stand 10 minutes before serving. Nutrition: Calories: 398, Fat: 17g, Saturated fat: 9g, Cholesterol: 164mg,

111.Provolone Stuffed Meatballs

Preparation time: 15 minutes Cooking time: 25 minutes Servings: 4

Ingredients:

1/2pound ground beef 1/2pound ground veal 1-pound ground pork 1/2cup breadcrumbs 2 tablespoons fresh parsley (minced) 1 egg (slightly beaten) 1/3 cup milk 3 cloves garlic, minced 1 teaspoon salt 1/2teaspoon ground black pepper 3 ounces provolone cheese, cut into cubes 2 tablespoons olive oil 2 cups marinara sauce 2 cups alfredo sauce 1-pound fettuccine pasta 1/4cup chopped fresh parsley for serving 1/2cup Parmesan cheese, grated, for serving

Directions

In a large bowl, mix together the beef, veal, pork, breadcrumbs, parsley, egg, milk, garlic, salt, and pepper. Mix with your hands to make sure it is completely blended. Form into meatballs, but do not overwork the meat or your meatballs will be tough. Press your thumb into the balls as you form them and place a cube of the cheese inside. Reform the meatball around it. In a heavy skillet, heat 2 teaspoons of olive oil over medium-high heat. When the oil is hot, add the meatballs, and brown them on all sides. When they are browned, transfer the balls to a plate line with paper towels to drain. (They will finish cooking in the sauce.) Transfer the meatballs to a medium-sized saucepan and add the marinara sauce. Cook over medium to low heat for about 25 minutes. Cook your fettuccine in a pot of boiling water until al dente, drain, and return to the pot. Add the Alfredo sauce. Heat and stir until the Alfredo sauce is hot. To serve, place a bed of the fettuccine with Alfredo sauce on a serving plate, and scoop on some meatballs with a bit of marinara over the top. Sprinkle with fresh parsley and Parmesan. Nutrition: Calories: 1550, Total Fat: 97g, Saturated Fat: 46g, Trans Fat: 2.5g, Cholesterol 0mg, Sodium: 3910mg, Total Carbohydrates: 113g, Dietary Fiber: 9g, Sugars: 0g, Protein: 58g

112. Taco Bell's Beef Chalupa

Preparation Time: 20 minutes Cooking Time: 25 minutes Servings: 6

Ingredients

For the Fry Bread 2 1/2cups all-purpose flour 1 tablespoon baking powder 1/2teaspoon salt 1 tablespoon vegetable shortening 1 cup milk For the Filling 1 tablespoon dried onion flakes 1/2cup water 1 pound ground beef 1/4cup flour 4 teaspoons chili powder 1 teaspoon paprika 1 teaspoon ground cumin 1 teaspoon salt 1/2teaspoon red pepper flakes Other Ingredients Oil for frying Sour cream, for serving Lettuce, for serving Grated cheese, for serving Chopped tomatoes, for serving

Directions

Prepare the dough. Combine the flour, baking powder, and salt. Cut in the shortening and mix in the milk. Do not overwork the dough. Cover the bowl and let the dough rest while you prepare the filling. Mix the onion flakes with the water and set them aside to hydrate. In a medium skillet brown the meat, breaking it into small pieces as it cooks. Drain any excess fat. Sprinkle the flour over the beef. Mix and let it cook for a minute or two. Add the onion bits and water. Stir in the spices and mix well. Turn the burner to a minimum and cover the skillet. Turn the fried dough out onto a lightly floured surface and divide it into 8 equal pieces. One at a time, roll them into circles. They should be 8–10 inches across and about a ¼-inch thick. If you want to fold the chalupa, use the rolling pin to press a flat space across the middle of the circle. Heat the oil. Pinch a small ball of dough (the size of a pea) and drop it in the oil. If the ball immediately floats to the surface, the oil is hot enough. One at a time, lower the dough circles into the oil. Use the tongs to press the dough under the oil, and cook on both sides until golden. Remove them to a plate lined with a paper towel. For folded chalupas, shape them while they're still hot. Add a portion of the meat filling and layer on the desired toppings. Nutrition: Calories 234 Carbs 2 g Fat 8.2 g Protein 12 g

113.   Mesa Grill's Crusted Filet Mignon

Preparation Time: 20 minutes Cooking Time: 8 minutes Servings: 4

Ingredients

Roasted Red Pepper and Ancho Salsa 2 ancho chiles 1/2cup boiling water 4 cloves garlic, chopped 2 tablespoons pine nuts 1 tablespoon honey 2 roasted red bell peppers, sliced in thin strips 2 tablespoons red wine vinegar 3 tablespoons chopped fresh cilantro leaves 1/2teaspoon salt 1/4teaspoon ground black pepper For the Steak 4 (8-ounce) filet mignon steaks 1 tablespoon vegetable oil 1/2teaspoon salt 4 teaspoons coarsely ground black pepper 8 ounces fresh goat cheese, cut into 4 slices Cilantro leaves, for garnish

Directions

Prepare the salsa. Pour the boiling water over the ancho chilies and let it sit for 1 hour. Remove the chilies from the water (keep the water) and chop the chilies, discarding the stems and seeds. Place them in a blender with 1/4cup of the soaking liquid, the garlic, pine nuts, and honey. Process until smooth. In a medium bowl, combine the purée with the bell peppers, red wine vinegar, cilantro, salt, and pepper. Cover the bowl and keep it at room temperature for 1 hour, or up to 4 hours. Heat the grill to medium-high. Clean and oil the grates. Brush the steaks with oil. Sprinkle both sides with salt, and press the peppercorns into one side of each steak. When the grill is hot, cook the steaks pepper side down for about 3 minutes, until the pepper is nicely charred. Flip the steaks over and cook them another 4 minutes or so on the other side (for medium-rare, internal temperature measures 135°F). In the final minute of cooking, place a slice of cheese on top of each steak, and allow it to melt a bit. Rest the steaks for 5–10 minutes before serving. Plate each steak and top with the Red Pepper Ancho salsa.
Nutrition: Calories 251 Carbs 2 g Fat 8.2 g Protein 12 g

114. Southwest Steak

Preparation Time: 20 minutes Cooking time: 10 minutes Servings: 2

Ingredients:

2 (6-ounce) sirloin steaks, or your favorite cut   2 teaspoons blackened steak seasoning 1/2cup red peppers, sliced 1/2cup green peppers, sliced 2 tablespoons unsalted butter 1 cup yellow onion, sliced 2 cloves garlic, minced Salt, to taste Pepper, to taste 2 slices cheddar cheese 2 slices Monterey jack cheese Vegetable medley or/and garlic mashed potatoes, for serving

Directions:

Preheat a cast iron (or another heavy skillet) or a grill.   Season the meat with steak seasoning and cook to your desired doneness (about 3–4 minutes on each side for medium-rare).   In another skillet, melt the butter and cook the peppers, onion, and garlic. Season with salt and pepper.   Just before the steak has reached your desired doneness, top with a slice of each cheese and cook a bit longer until the cheese melts.   Serve the steaks with pepper and onion mix and garlic mashed potatoes.   Nutrition: Calories: 350 Total Fat: 17g Carbs: 34g Protein: 14g Fiber: 2g

115. Outback Style Steak

Preparation Time: 40 minutes Cooking time: 10 minutes Servings: 4

Ingredients:

4 (6-ounce) sirloin or ribeye steaks   2 tablespoons olive oil   2 tablespoons Old Bay Seasoning 2 tablespoons brown sugar 1 teaspoon garlic powder 1 teaspoon salt 1/2teaspoon black pepper 1/2teaspoon onion powder 1/2teaspoon ground cumin

Directions: Take the steaks out of the fridge and let them sit at room temperature for about 20 minutes.   Combine all the seasonings and mix well.   Rub the steaks with oil and some of the spice mixture, covering all the surfaces. Let the steaks sit for 20–30 minutes.   Meanwhile, heat your grill to medium-high.   Cook the steaks for about 5 minutes on each side for medium rare (or to an internal temperature of 130°F.) Let them sit for 5 minutes before serving.   Nutrition: Calories: 254 Total Fat: 13g Carbs: 56g Protein: 45g Fiber: 3g

116. Bacon Cheeseburger

Servings: 6-8 Preparation Time: 15 minutes Cooking Time: 30-35 minutes

Ingredients

1 pizza crust of choice 1/2-3/4 cup basic or marinara sauce 4 strips bacon 1/2 pound hamburger 1/2 small onion chopped Salt and pepper, to taste 1 1/2 cup mozzarella 1/2 cup cheddar, shredded 1/2 tomato sliced or chopped

Directions

Preheat oven 425 degrees F. Heat bacon strips in skillet or non-stick frying pan over medium heat until browned and almost crisp. Cool and chop into bite size pieces. Set aside. Drain off any bacon drippings in excess of 2 Tablespoons. If needed, add a bit of olive oil. Add the hamburger meat and bacon. Season with salt and pepper. Stir-fry until browned. Remove from heat and let cool. Spread sauce over crust and spread with cheddar cheese. Spread hamburger mixture on top. Sprinkle with shredded mozzarella and top with chopped bacon. Bake until golden brown and bubbly (12-15 minutes). Nutrition: Calories 376 Carbs 42 g Fat 14 g Protein 23 g Sodium 1332 mg

117. Meat with Mushrooms, Bell Pepper & Olives

Servings: 8 Preparation Time: 20 minutes Cooking Time: 20-30 minutes

Ingredients

1 pizza crust of choice 1/2 cup marinara sauce 2 cups mozzarella, freshly shredded 2 pounds combination of seasoned meat (pork and beef), Italian sausage, pepperoni, and ham 1/2 cup mushrooms, sliced thinly 1 medium green bell pepper, sliced into rings 1 red onion, sliced 1/4 cup black olives, pitted and sliced

Directions

Preheat oven to 425 degrees F. Brown the meat and sausage in a little oil over medium heat until browned. Slice the ham. Spread sauce over crust. and sprinkle with cheese. Top with seasoned meat, sausage, ham, pepperoni, mushrooms, bell pepper, onion and olives. Bake until golden brown (about 20 minutes). Nutrition: Calories 470 Carbs 27 g Fat 28 g Protein 25 g Sodium 827 mg

118. Chi Chi's Pork Tenderloin

Preparation time: 10 minutes Cooking time: 15 minutes Servings: 12

Ingredients

2 pounds pork tenderloin Chi Chi's Bourbon Marinade 10 ounces Chi Chi's diced tomatoes with green chilies, drained 1/3 cup bourbon 1/3 cup soy sauce 1/3 cup Worcestershire sauce 1 small yellow onion, chopped 2 tablespoons honey 2 tablespoons mustard 1/2teaspoon red pepper flakes

Directions

Combine the ingredients for the marinade and place it in a resealable bag. Add the pork and turn to coat. Refrigerate for 8 hours or overnight, turning it from time to time. Preheat the grill or broiler to medium. Remove the meat from the marinade, reserving the marinade. Grill or broil the meat for 7 minutes on each side, or until it reaches 165°F internally. Strain the marinade into a saucepan and bring it to a boil. Simmer for 2–3 minutes and strain. Serve it as a sauce with the meat. Nutrition: Calories 251 Carbs 2 g Fat 8.2 g Protein 10.3 g

119. Grilled Pork Chops

Preparation Time: 20 minutes Cooking Time: 10 minutes Servings: 4

Ingredients: 1/4 cup kosher salt 1/4 cup sugar 2 cups water 2 cups ice water 4 center-cut pork rib chops (1 inch thick and 8 ounces each) 2 tablespoons canola oil Basic Rub: 3 tablespoons paprika 1 teaspoon each garlic powder, onion powder, ground cumin and ground mustard 1 teaspoon coarsely ground pepper 1/2 teaspoon ground chipotle pepper

DirectionsIn a large saucepan, combine salt, sugar and 2 cups water; cook and stir over medium heat until salt and sugar are dissolved. Remove from heat. Add 2 cups ice water to cool brine to room temperature. Place pork chops in a large resealable plastic bag; add cooled brine. Seal bag, pressing out as much air as possible; turn to coat chops. Place in a 13x9-in. baking dish. Refrigerate 8-12 hours. Remove chops from brine, rinse, and pat dry. Discard brine. Brush both sides of chops with oil. In a small bowl, mix rub ingredients; rub over pork chops. Let stand at room temperature 30 minutes. Grill chops on an oiled rack, covered, over medium heat 4-6 minutes on each side or until a thermometer reads 145°. Let stand 5 minutes before serving. Nutrition: Calories: 300, Fat: 18g, Cholesterol: 72mg, Sodium: 130mg, Carbohydrate: 5g, Protein: 30g

120. Moe's Southwestern Grill's Taco Pie

Preparation Time: 10 minutes Cooking Time: 35 minutes Servings: 4

Ingredients

1 1/2cups crushed tortilla chips 2 teaspoons taco seasoning 3 tablespoons butter, melted 3 cups leftover taco beef 1 1/2cups refried beans 1 cup spicy salsa 1 cup grated cheddar cheese Cherry tomatoes, halved Topping Salsa Sour cream or crema Chopped salad

Directions

Preheat the oven to 450°F. In a mixing bowl, combine the crushed tortilla chips, taco seasoning, and melted butter. Mix well and press the crust into a 9-inch pie plate. Bake for 10 minutes. Reduce the oven temperature to 375°F. Spoon the taco beef into the crust and spread the refried beans on it. Layer the salsa on top, and then the grated cheddar. Scatter the tomatoes on top. Bake for 20 minutes, switching to broil in the final few minutes to ensure the cheese is melted and lightly browned. Cool the pie for 10 minutes before slicing. Serve with favorite toppings. Nutrition: Calories 221 Carbs 2 g Fat 8.2 g Protein 12 g

121.   Taco Bell's Enchiritos

Preparation Time: 20 minutes Cooking Time: 15 minutes Servings: 12

Ingredients

Seasoning 1/4cup all-purpose flour 1 tablespoon chili powder 1 teaspoon salt 1/2teaspoon dried onion flakes 1/2teaspoon paprika 1/4teaspoon onion powder 1 dash garlic powder Tortillas filling 1 pound lean ground beef 1/2cup water 1 (16-ounce) can refried beans 12 small flour tortillas 1/2cup onion, diced 1(16-ounce) can red chili sauce 2 cups cheddar cheese, shredded Some green onions, for serving Some sour cream, for serving

Directions

Mix all the seasoning ingredients in a bowl. Coat the beef in the seasoning using your hands. Make sure that the beef fully absorbs the flavor from the spices. Brown the seasoned beef in the water over medium heat, for 8 to 10 minutes. Stir the beef occasionally to remove lumps. While the beef is browning, microwave the beans on high for 2 minutes. Wrap the tortillas in a wet towel and microwave for 1 minute. When the beef is done, assemble the tortillas a) Place some beans in the middle of the tortilla; b) Place some beef on top, add some onion; c) Roll up the tortilla by bringing both ends together in the center; d) Place the tortilla in a microwave-safe casserole; and e) Spread the chili sauce and cheddar cheese on top of the tortilla. Repeat step 5 until the casserole is full. Heat the entire dish in the microwave for 2-3 minutes. The dish is done when the cheese melts. Serve with green onions and sour cream, if desired. Nutrition: Calories 256 Carbs 12 g Fat 13.2 g Protein 12 g

DESSERTS RECIPES

Desserts Recipes

122.   Triple Chocolate Meltdown

Preparation Time: 1 hour Cooking time: 30 minutes Servings: 8

Ingredients:

2 cups heavy cream, divided   1 cup white chocolate chips   1 cup semi-sweet chocolate chips   1-pound bittersweet chocolate, chopped   1/2cup butter, softened   6 eggs   1 1/2cups of sugar   1 1/2cups all-purpose flour   Ice cream, for serving

Directions:

Preheat the oven to 400°F.   Prepare 8 ramekins by first coating the inside with butter then sprinkling them with flour so the bottom and sides are covered. Place them on a baking tray.   In a saucepan, bring 1 cup of heavy cream to a simmer. Remove it from the heat and add the white chocolate chips, stirring until the chocolate is melted and the mixture is smooth. Allow it to cool for about a half an hour, stirring occasionally.   Repeat with the other cup of cream and the semi-sweet chocolate chips.   In a double boiler, combine the bittersweet chocolate with the softened butter and stir until the chocolate is melted and the mixture is smooth. Remove the bowl from the heat and allow it to cool for about 10 minutes   In a mixing bowl, beat the eggs and the sugar together for about 2 minutes, or until the mixture is foamy. Use a rubber spatula to fold in the bittersweet chocolate mixture.   Turn the mixer to low and beat in the flour half a cup at a time, being careful not to overmix the batter.   Pour the batter evenly into the prepared ramekins and place the baking tray in oven. Bake for about 18 minutes.   When done, the cakes should have a slight crust but still be soft in the middle. Remove them from oven when they have reached this look. If you cook them too long you won't get the lava cake effect.   Let the ramekins sit on the tray for 2–3 minutes and then invert them onto serving plates. Drizzle some of both the semi-sweet and white chocolate sauces over the top and serve with a scoop of ice cream.   Nutrition: Calories: 421 Fat: 13 g Carbs: 22 g Protein: 24.0 g Sodium: 311 mg

.

123. Chocolate Pecan Pie

Preparation Time: 10 minutes Cooking time: 50 minutes Servings: 8

Ingredients:

3 eggs 1/2cup sugar 1 cup corn syrup 1/2teaspoon salt 1 teaspoon vanilla extract 1/4cup melted butter 1 cup pecans 3 tablespoons semisweet chocolate chips 1 unbaked pie shell

Directions:

Preheat the oven to 350°F. Beat together the eggs and sugar in a mixing bowl, then add the corn syrup, salt, vanilla and butter. Put the chocolate chips and pecans inside the pie shell and pour the egg mixture over the top. Bake for 50–60 minutes or until set. Serve with vanilla ice cream. Nutrition: Calories: 483 Fat: 13.8 g Carbs: 22. 2 g Protein: 29.7 g Sodium: 154 mg

124. Classic Cheesecake from The Cheesecake Factory

Preparation Time: 4 hours 15 minutes Cooking Time: 1 hour 5 minutes Servings: 12

Ingredients Crust: 11/2cups of graham cracker crumbs 1/4teaspoon of cinnamon, ground 1/3 cup of margarine, melted Filling: 4 8-ounce of packages cream cheese, softened 11/4cups of white sugar 1/2cup of sour cream 2 teaspoons of vanilla extract 5 large eggs Topping: 1/2cup of sour cream 2 teaspoons of sugar

Directions Preheat oven to 475°F and warmth an outsized skillet with 1/2inch water inside. Combine ingredients for the crust in a bowl and prepare a large pie pan lined with parchment paper, spread crust onto the pan, and press firmly. Cover with foil and confine freezer until able to use. Combine ingredients for the filling, apart from eggs, in a bowl. Scrape bowl while beating until the mixture is smooth. Mix in eggs and beat until thoroughly blended. Take out crust from the freezer and add filling onto crust, spreading evenly. Place the pie pan into a heated water bath (skillet in the oven) and bake for about 12 minutes. Reduce heat to 350 °F. still bake for about 50 minutes or until the cake top is golden. Remove from oven and transfer skillet onto a wire rack to chill. Prepare the topping by mixing all ingredients in a bowl. Coat cake with topping, then cover. Keep inside the refrigerator for a minimum of 4 hours. Serve cold. Nutrition: Calories: 519, Total Fat: 39 g, Carbs: 34 g, Protein: 10 g, Sodium: 423 mg

125.   Peach Cobbler

Preparation Time: 10 minutes Cooking time: 45 minutes Servings: 4

Ingredients:

11/4cups Bisquick   1 cup milk   1/2cup melted butter   1/4teaspoon nutmeg   1/2teaspoon cinnamon   Vanilla ice cream, for serving   Filling: 1 (30-ounce) can peaches in syrup, drained   1/4cup sugar   Topping: 1/2cup brown sugar   1/4cup almond slices   1/2teaspoon cinnamon   1 tablespoon melted butter

Directions:

Preheat the oven to 375°F.   Grease the bottom and sides of an 8×8-inch pan.   Whisk together the Bisquick, milk, butter, nutmeg and cinnamon in a large mixing bowl. When thoroughly combined, pour into the greased baking pan.   Mix together the peaches and sugar in another mixing bowl. Put the filling on top of the batter in the pan. Bake for about 45 minutes.   In another bowl, mix together the brown sugar, almonds, cinnamon, and melted butter. After the cobbler has cooked for 45 minutes, cover evenly with the topping and bake for an additional 10 minutes.   Serve with a scoop of vanilla ice cream.   Nutrition: Calories: 446 Fat: 12.6 g Carbs: 21. 2 g Protein: 21.1 g Sodium: 300 mg

126.   Molten Chocolate Cake

Preparation Time: 1 hour 30 minutes Cooking Time: 30 minutes Servings: 10

Ingredients:

1 Duncan Hines fudge cake mix   3 large eggs   1 cup milk   1/2cup oil   1/2cup sour cream   Vanilla ice cream   Chocolate shell ice cream topping   Caramel sauce   For Magic Shell 1/4cup coconut oil   2 cups chocolate chips, semi-sweet   For Hot Fudge 1 bag semi-sweet chocolate chips (12-ounces)   4 tablespoons unsalted butter   1 can sweetened condensed milk (14-ounces)   A pinch of salt   1 teaspoon pure vanilla extract

Directions:

Stir the dry cake mix together with sour cream, eggs, milk & oil in a large bowl.   Lightly coat a large-sized cupcake pan with the nonstick spray & distribute the batter evenly approximately 3/4 full. Bake as per the directions mentioned on the package.   Turn the cakes out onto their tops creating a "volcano" & let cool.   Gently cut a hole out of the middle without going clear to the bottom using a pairing or serrated knife.   Fill with cool hot fudge & then slice off the bottom circle of the piece of cake you removed and place it on the hot fudge hole like a lid.   Using a plastic wrap; cover & let chill in a fridge for 30 minutes.   Remove the cakes from freezer & reheat in the microwave for half a minute, until warm.   Top with caramel, ice cream & magic shell.   For Magic Shell: Place the chocolate along with the coconut oil in a microwave safe bowl and slowly heat for 30 second intervals until melted, stirring often.   Serve over cold ice cream & it would harden.   For Hot Fudge: Melt the entire ingredients together over medium heat in a medium saucepan.   Bring the mixture to a boil, stirring every now and then. Continue to boil & stir for a minute or two more. Remove the pan from heat & continue to stir for a minute. Let the fudge sauce to cool.   Nutrition: Calories: 441 Fat: 12.2 g Carbs: 24. 1 g Protein: 23.3 g Sodium: 208 mg

127. DIY Pumpkin Scones

Preparation Time: 5 minutes Cooking Time: 10 minutes Servings: 2

Ingredients:

Scones: 2 cups all-purpose flour 1/3 cup brown sugar 1 teaspoon cinnamon 1 teaspoon baking powder 3/4 teaspoon cloves, ground 1/2teaspoon ginger, ground 1/2teaspoon nutmeg, ground 1/2teaspoon baking soda 1/4teaspoon salt 1/2cup unsalted butter, cut into cubes (keep cold) 1/2cup pumpkin puree 3 tablespoons milk 1 large egg 2 teaspoons vanilla extract Flour, for rolling dough Glaze: 1 cup powdered sugar - 2 tablespoons Spiced glaze: - 1 cup powdered sugar 1/4teaspoon cinnamon - 1/4teaspoon cloves, ground 1/4teaspoon ginger, ground Pinch nutmeg - 2 tablespoons milk

Directions:

Preheat oven to 400°F and prepare a baking tray lined with parchment paper. Mix flour, sugar, cinnamon, baking powder, cloves, ginger, nutmeg, baking soda, and salt in a bowl. Using your fingers, incorporate cold butter into the bowl until mixture is crumbly. Stir together pumpkin puree, milk, egg, and vanilla in another bowl. Add to dry ingredients and mix until mixture becomes a soft dough. Sprinkle a flat surface with flour. Transfer dough onto surface and knead for about 3 minutes. Flatten dough with a rolling pin into a large rectangle, about 1 inch thick and 10 by 7 inches. Cut in a cross to make 4 equal rectangles, then cut each rectangle diagonally. This makes 8 triangles. Transfer dough onto baking tray, careful to keep triangles from touching. Bake for about 10 minutes or until baked through. Prepare the glaze by mixing ingredients in a bowl until smooth. Do the same in a separate bowl for the spiced glaze. Allow scones to cool for about 10 minutes. Coat with glaze, then drip spiced glaze on top in zigzags. Allow glazes to set before serving. Nutrition: Calories: 460, Carbohydrates: 65g, Protein: 6g, Fat: 19g, Saturated Fat: 9g, Cholesterol: 37mg, Sodium: 225mg, Potassium: 396mg, Fiber: 3g, Sugar: 20g

128. Maple Butter Blondie

Preparation Time: 15 minutes Cooking time: 35 minutes Servings: 9

Ingredients:

1/3 cup butter, melted   1 cup brown sugar, packed   1 large egg, beaten   1 tablespoon vanilla extract   1/2teaspoon baking powder   1/8teaspoon baking soda   1/8teaspoon salt   1 cup flour   2/3cup white chocolate chips   1/3 cup pecans, chopped (or walnuts)   Maple butter sauce   3/4 cup maple syrup   1/2cup butter   3/4 cup brown sugar   8 ounces' cream cheese, softened to room temp   1/4cup pecans, chopped   Vanilla ice cream, for serving

Directions:

Preheat the oven to 350°F and coat a 9x9 baking pan with cooking spray.   In a mixing bowl, combine the butter, brown sugar, egg, and vanilla, and beat until smooth.   Sift in the baking powder, baking soda, salt, and flour, and stir until it is well incorporated. Fold in the white chocolate chips.   Bake for 20–25 minutes.   While those are in the oven, prepare the maple butter sauce by combining the maple syrup and butter in a medium saucepan.   Cook over low heat until the butter is melted. Add the brown sugar and cream cheese. Stir constantly until the cream cheese has completely melted, then remove the pot from the heat.   Remove the blondies from the oven and cut them into squares.   Top with vanilla ice cream, maple butter sauce, and chopped nuts. Nutrition: Calories: 354 Fat: 12 g Carbs: 201 g Protein: 24.0 g Sodium: 231 mg

129. Cinnamon Apple Turnover

Preparation Time: 10 minutes Cooking time: 25 minutes Servings: 6

Ingredients:

1 large Granny Smith apple, peeled, cored, and diced 1/2teaspoon cornstarch 1/4teaspoon cinnamon Dash ground nutmeg 1/4cup brown sugar 1/4cup applesauce 1/4teaspoon vanilla extract 1 tablespoon butter, melted 1 sheet of puff pastry, thawed Whipped cream or vanilla ice cream, to serve

Directions:

Preheat the oven to 400°F. Prepare a baking sheet by spraying it with non-stick cooking spray or using a bit of oil on a paper towel. In a mixing bowl, mix together the apples, cornstarch, cinnamon, nutmeg, and brown sugar. Stir to make sure the apples are well covered with the spices. Then stir in the applesauce and the vanilla. Lay out your puff pastry and cut it into squares. You should be able to make 4 or 6 depending on how big you want your turnovers to be and how big your pastry is. Place some of the apple mixture in the center of each square and fold the corners of the pastry up to make a pocket. Pinch the edges together to seal. Then brush a bit of the melted butter over the top to give the turnovers that nice brown color. Place the filled pastry onto the prepared baking pan and transfer to the preheated oven. Bake 20–25 minutes, or until they become a golden brown in color. Serve with whipped cream or vanilla ice cream. Nutrition: Calories: 235 Fat: 15.8 g Carbs: 20. 5 g Protein: 26 g Sodium: 109 mg

130. Cinnabon's Classic Cinnamon Rolls

Preparation Time: 2 hours 45 minutes Cooking Time: 15 minutes Servings: 12

Ingredients

Dough: 1 cup of warm milk (about 110 °F) 2 eggs 1/3 cup of margarine, melted 4 1/2cups of white bread flour 1 teaspoon of salt 1/2cup of white sugar 2 1/2teaspoons of rapid rising yeast 1 tablespoon of all-purpose flour 1 cup of brown sugar 2 1/2tablespoons of cinnamon, ground 1/3 cup butter, softened Frosting: 3 ounces of cream cheese, softened 1/4cup of butter softened 1 1/2cups of powdered sugar 1/2teaspoon of vanilla extract 1/8teaspoon of salt

Directions

Arrange dough ingredients in the bread machine pan following the manufacturer's instructions. Select the dough cycle and press Start. Once the dough has reached twice its original size, transfer onto a surface and lightly sprinkled with flour. Cover, and put aside for 10 minutes. Preheat oven to 400 °F. Mix sugar and cinnamon in a bowl. Flatten dough into an outsized rectangle, about 16 by 21 inches. Brush with 1/3 cup butter and sugar and cinnamon mixture. Roll dough onto itself in a roll and slice through 12 even pieces. Transfer slices onto an outsized baking sheet. Cover and let rest for a half-hour or until the size has doubled. Bake for quarter-hour or until lightly brown. To make the frosting, combine all ingredients in a bowl. Mix until smooth. Remove rolls from oven and drizzle with frosting. Serve. Nutrition: Calories 525, Total Fat 19 g, Carbs 82 g, Protein 9 g, Sodium 388 mg

131. P.F. Chang's Coconut Pineapple Ice Cream with Banana Spring Rolls

Preparation Time: 5 minutes Cooking time 30 minutes Servings 6

Ingredients

Ice cream 1 (13½-ounce) jar of coconut milk 1 cup of granulated sugar 1 1/2 cups of heavy cream 1 teaspoon of coconut extract 1 (8-ounce) can of crushed pineapple, drained 1/3 cup of shredded coconut Banana spring rolls 3 ripe bananas, preferably plantains, halved horizontally 3 rice paper or wonton wrappers 1–3 tablespoons of brown sugar 1 teaspoon of cinnamon Oil, for frying - Caramel sauce, for drizzling (optional) - Paste for sealing wrappers 2 tablespoons of water - 2 teaspoons of flour or cornstarch

Directions

Make the frozen dessert. Place coconut milk and sugar in a bowl. Mix with mixer until sugar is dissolved. Mix in remaining ingredients until well-blended. Place in frozen dessert maker to churn and follow manufacturer's instructions until frozen dessert holds when scooped with a spoon, about a half-hour. Transfer to a container with lid and freeze for a minimum of 2 hours or until desired firmness is reached. Make the banana spring rolls. Lay the wrapper on a flat surface. Position a banana slice near the sting of the wrapper closest to you at rock bottom. Sprinkle with about one teaspoon to 1 tablespoon sugar, depending on how sweet you would like it. Sprinkle with a pinch or two of cinnamon. Roll up sort of a burrito, tucking in the sides. In a small bowl, stir the paste ingredients together. Brush the paste on the sting of the wrapper and seal the roll. Place roll, closed side down, on a plate, and repeat with the remaining bananas. Heat oil, about 1–1 1/2 inches deep, over medium to high heat. Fry the rolls until golden brown, about 1–2 minutes on all sides. Place on paper towels to empty. Serve the rolls with scoops of frozen dessert and drizzle with caramel sauce, if desired. Nutrition: Calories: 940 Total Fat: 35g Carbs: 14g Protein: 149g Fiber:2g

132.   Campfire S'mores

Preparation Time: 15 minutes Cooking time: 40 minutes Servings: 9

Ingredients:

Graham Cracker Crust   2 cups graham cracker crumbs   1/4cup sugar
1/2cup butter   1/2teaspoon cinnamon   1 small package brownie mix
(enough for an 8×8-inch pan), or use the brownie ingredients listed
below.   Brownie Mix: 1/2cup flour - 1/3 cup cocoa   1/4teaspoon baking
powder   1/4teaspoon salt   1/2cup butter   1 cup sugar   1 teaspoon vanilla - 2
large eggs   S'mores Topping: 9 large marshmallows - 5 Hershey candy
bars - 41/2cups vanilla ice cream   1/2cup chocolate sauce

Directions:

Preheat the oven to 350°F.   Mix together the graham cracker crumbs, sugar,
cinnamon and melted butter in a medium bowl. Stir until the crumbs and
sugar have combined with the butter.   Line an 8×8-inch baking dish with
parchment paper. Make sure to use enough so that you'll be able to lift the
baked brownies out of the dish easily. Press the graham cracker mixture into
the bottom of the lined pan.   Place pan in the oven to prebake the crust a bit
while you are making the brownie mixture.   Melt the butter over medium
heat in a large saucepan, then stir in the sugar and vanilla. Whisk in the eggs
one at a time. Then whisk in the dry ingredients, followed by the nuts. Mix
until smooth. Take the crust out of the oven, pour the mixture into it, and
bake for 23–25 minutes. When brownies are done, remove from oven and let
cool in the pan.   After the brownies have cooled completely, lift them out of
the pan using the edges of the parchment paper. Be careful not to crack or
break the brownies. Cut into individual slices.   When you are ready to serve,
place a marshmallow on top of each brownie and broil in the oven until the
marshmallow starts to brown. You can also microwave for a couple of
seconds, but you won't get the browning that you would in the
broiler.   Remove from the oven and top each brownie with half of a Hershey
bar. Serve with ice cream and a drizzle of chocolate sauce.   Nutrition:
Calories: 623 Fat: 14.8 g Carbs: 10. 2 g Protein: 39.0 g Sodium: 231 mg

133.   Baked Apple Dumplings

Preparation Time: 20 minutes Cooking time: 40 minutes Servings: 4

Ingredients:

1 (171/2ounce) package frozen puff pastry, thawed   1 cup sugar   6
tablespoons dry breadcrumbs   2 teaspoons ground cinnamon   1 pinch
ground nutmeg   1 egg, beaten   4 Granny Smith apples, peeled, cored and
halved   Vanilla ice cream for serving   Icing: 1 cup confectioners' sugar   1
teaspoon vanilla extract   3 tablespoons milk   Pecan Streusel: 2/3cup
chopped toasted pecans   2/3cup packed brown sugar   2/3cup all-purpose
flour   5 tablespoons melted butter

Directions:

Preheat oven to 425 ° F. When the puff pastry is completely thawed, unfold
each sheet to measure 12 inches by 12 inches. Cut the leaves into quarters.
Combine sugar, crumbs, cinnamon, and nutmeg in a bowl. Brush one of the
puff pastry squares with some of the beaten eggs. Add about 1 tablespoon of
bread mixture on top, then add half an apple, core down, over the crumbs.
Add another tablespoon of bread mix Seal the dough by pulling on the
corners and squeezing the dough until the seams are completely sealed.
Repeat this process with the other squares. Collect ingredients for stressful
pecans in a small bowl Grease a baking sheet or line it with parchment. Lay
the bouquets on the sheet and brush with a little more beaten egg. Top with
sterile walnuts. Reduce temperature to 350 ° F after baking for 15 minutes
and bake for an additional 25 minutes or until lightly browned. Prepare the
frosting by combining the sugar, vanilla, and pastry milk until it reaches the
proper consistency. Nutrition: Calories: 214 Fat: 10 g Carbs: 14 g Protein: 21
g Sodium: 206 mg

134. Asparagus & Lemon Bruschetta

Preparation Time: 5 minutes Cooking Time: 10 minutes Servings: 2

Ingredients:

5 bruschetta toast, prepared 5 tablespoons cheese & prosciutto spread 1/4 cup asparagus, cooked & sliced 2 tablespoons chive and lemon vinaigrette 5 bits lemon zest Cheese & Prosciutto Spread: 1/4 cup ricotta cheese 1 1/3 Oz cheese, room temperature 1 1/3 Oz mascarpone cheese 1/4 cup prosciutto cheese 1/4 teaspoon garlic puree 1/2 tablespoon lemon juice Pinch of salt & pepper Chive & Lemon Vinaigrette: 1 1/2 tablespoons corn syrup 4 tablespoons lemon juice 1 tablespoon chives, chopped 3/4 cup vegetable oil Pinch salt & pepper

Directions:

To make the vinaigrette: Combine the corn syrup and lemon juice in a food processor for 1 minute. Turn the blender to high speed and pour vegetable oil slowly through the top of the blender until it is fully integrated. Add Chives, then mix for 2 seconds. Set it aside for assembly. The cheese spread preparation: blend the ricotta cheese and cream cheese in a small mixer for 4-5 minutes or until smooth at speed 2. Add the mascarpone cheese, garlic puree, and prosciutto, then blend for 1 or 2 minutes more. Put aside for assembly. To assemble the bruschetta: Par cook toast in the oven at 525 degrees for 1 minute or until golden brown. Put 1 lb. of the cheese and spread the prosciutto on each slice of toast. Melt the cheese on the bruschetta for 2 1/2 minutes or until golden brown, in a 525-degree oven. Put it into your serving plate. Mix the sliced asparagus and 1 tablespoon of lemon vinaigrette, lemon zest, and salt and pepper season in a small mixing cup. Place the toast on top of each bruschetta – piling it high and clean. Drizzle 1 spoonful of lemon vinaigrette around and over the toast. Nutrition: Calories: 592, Total Fat: 42g Cholesterol: 138mg, Sodium: 436mg, Potassium: 270mg,

OTHER RESTAURANT FAVOURITES RECIPES

135. McDonald's Fries

Preparation Time: 6 minutes Cooking time: 5 minutes Servings: 4

Ingredients:

Canola Oil Soybean oil (can substitute safflower oil) Corn oil 1/4cup ice 1/2teaspoon baking powder 1/2cup unsalted beef stock 1/4cup of soy milk 1 bag of shoestring potatoes (26 ounces)

Directions:

Heat oil to 375 degrees F. In a cup, add the ice, beef stock, soy milk and baking powder, and mix until combined. Place the fries in the brine, then remove them after a few seconds. Then you place five minutes of brined fries back in the freezer. Put the fries into the oil and cook for 2 minutes or until the desired doneness hits. Remove, and have fun! Nutrition: Calories: 388 Fat: 21g Fiber: 5 Carbs: 30g Protein: 12g

136. McDonald's Grilled Burger

Preparation Time: 10 minutes Cooking time: 10 minutes Servings: 4

Ingredients:

1/2 cup maple syrup One batch of pancake batter Four strips of bacon that is cooked and cut in half (or use can use4 cooked pork sausage patties) 4 slices American cheese 4 eggs

Directions:

If you have one, line up a baking sheet with parchment paper or a Silpat before starting the maple sugar. Deposit back. Pour the syrup into a small saucepan and place over medium heat. Bring to simmer, with regular stirring. When it starts boiling slowly, make sure that you keep stirring to prevent it from getting stuck to the bowl. Test the temperature after a minute, if you have a thermometer. Once the syrup hits around 230oF, it will start to "calm down" and become less frightening like a fire. You will also note it is getting slightly darker. Two-three minutes later: once it has become very dim, remove it from heat just as you detect a twinge of caramel-smell. At that point, the thermometer should be 265oF. Pour the maple syrup out and spread thinly onto your lined baking sheet. Do not touch it. It's (almost) hot as molten lead. Let's let it cool. If you want in a hurry, pop it up in the fridge. When it's fine, you can peel it in pieces off the paper and break it up by smashing it in some way. Phew, yeah. That is over. Now right on to the pancakes. Make a single batch of my recipe for pancake, or any recipe that would produce eight pancakes. If you use round molds for your pancakes, add a little butter to the insides. Heat your griddle to hot over low heat. Smear some butter on it and put as many pancake molds on the griddle as you can. Put two tablespoons of batter into each of these, top with some maple crystals, add two more tablespoons. The idea is to sandwich the crystals inside the pancakes so as not to spread maple sugar around your grid and be a hassle. Cook until there are bubbles around the edges and the edges of the cakes appear fried. Remove the tongs from the rings, and turn the cakes. Cook 1-2 more minutes until done. Top with a cheese plate, scrambled or fried egg, bacon or sausage, and a pancake. Eat it right away! Or you can also cool it down and freeze for a rainy day. Nutrition: Calories: 467 Fat: 27g Fiber: 3 Car

137.   IHOP Crepe

Preparation Time: 10 minutes Cooking Time: 20 minutes Servings: 4

Ingredients: 1 cup of all-purpose flour 2 eggs 1/2 cup of milk 1/4 teaspoon of salt 1/2 cup of water 2 tablespoon of melted butter

Directions: Mix the flour and eggs in a bowl until combined.   Add milk and water and then mix again until evenly combined.   Finally, finish off the batter with butter and salt applied.   Keep whisking until the batter gets smooth.   Heat a non-stick saucepan and add the butter.   When the butter has heated a little, ladle some of the batter over it.   Spread the batter slightly by tilting the pan, and cook the bottom side until golden brown.   Now, turn the crepe onto the other side to get the same color.   Do the same with all the crepes, and serve soft. Nutrition: Calories: 1120; Fat: 75g: Carbs: 52g: Protein: 60g

138.   IHOP Strawberry & Cream Crepes

Preparation Time: 25 minutes Cooking Time: 1 hour Servings: 22 crepes

Ingredients: 1-1/2 cups of milk 3 big eggs   2 tablespoons of butter, thawed 1/2 teaspoon of lemon extract 1-1/4 cups of all-purpose flour   2 tablespoons of sweets Dash salt Topping: 1/2 cup of sugar   2 tablespoon of corn starch   3/4 cup of water   1 tablespoon of lemon extract 1 teaspoon of strawberry extract 1/4 teaspoon of red food coloring, optional   4 mugs of cut fresh strawberries.   Filling: 1 cup of heavy whipping cream   1 package deal (8 ounces) lotion cheese, relaxed.   2 cups of confectioners' sugar 1 teaspoon of vanilla essence **Directions:**In a large bowl, mix the milk, eggs, butter and extract.   Mix the salt, flour and glucose; add to milk mixture and blend well. Cover and cool it for 1 hour.   Heat up an 8-in, gently oiled non-stick skillet; pour in 2 tablespoons of the mix right into middle of the skillet. Turn and lift the frying pan to base plate in equal measure.   Cook until the top looks dry; turn over and cook for 15–20 seconds. Repeat with the remaining mix and grease the skillet as required. In between, stack crepes when cold, with polished paper or paper towels.   In a tiny pan, mix glucose and corn starch; rouse in water and lemon extract until smooth. Cook and rouse for 1 minute or until expanded. Add strawberries. In a small bowl, blend the mix up until stiff optimal develop; reserved.   In a sizable bowl, mix the cream cheese, confectioners' sugar and vanilla up until smooth; crease in beat cream. Spoon 2 rounded tablespoons of this mix on the center of each crepe. Top with strawberry topping.   Nutrition: Calories: 800; Fat: 30g; Carbs: 117g; Protein: 19g

139. Perkins Restaurant & Bakery Chocolate Silk Pie

Cooking Time: 28 minutes Preparation Time: 25 minutes Servings: 2

Ingredients:

1 (9 inches) pie crust - 1 jar (7 oz.) of marshmallow crème   1 cup of semisweet chocolate chips   1/4cup of butter, cubed - 2 oz. unsweetened chocolate   2 tablespoons of strong brewed coffee   1 cup of heavy whipping cream, whipped   Topping: 1 cup of heavy whipping cream - 2 tablespoons of powdered sugar   Chocolate curls, optional

Directions:

Spread the pie crust in a 9-inches pie plate and cut off the edges extending half-inch beyond the rim of the pie plate; refrigerate this crust for 30 minutes until all other ingredients are ready.   Set the oven's temperature to 425°F for preheating; Cover the crust with a thick foil sheet and add some uncooked rice or dried beans for weight. Bake this crust on the lower rack of the oven for 25 minutes; once baked, remove the foil from the crust and bake again for 3 minutes. Transfer this crust to a wire rack and allow it to cool; Place a heavy saucepan over low heat and add chocolate chips, butter, unsweetened chocolate, coffee, and marshmallow crème. Stir until the chocolate is melted and mix well with other ingredients. Remove this mixture from the heat and fold in whipped cream. Mix well and pour this filling into the baked crust. Prepare the topping by beating the cream with powdered sugar in a mixing bowl until it forms peaks. Spread the cream topping over the pie and cover it with plastic wrap. Place the pie in the refrigerator for 3 hours. Garnish with chocolate curls and shavings. Slice and serve.   Nutrition: Calories: 760; Fat: 66g; Carbs: 54g; Protein: 6g Perkins

140. Coco's Bakery Restaurant Santa Fe Quiche

Preparation Time: 15minutes Cooking Time: 55 minutes Servings: 6

Ingredients:

3 large eggs, beaten   1 pastry shell (9 inches), unbaked   1/4 teaspoon of pepper   1 can (2-1/4 ounces) of sliced ripe olives, drained   1 cup of shredded Monterey Jack cheese   1-1/2 cups of half-and-half cream   1 teaspoon of salt   1 teaspoon of chili powder   1 tablespoon of all-purpose flour   1 cup of shredded cheddar cheese   1 can (4 ounces) of chopped green chilies, well drained

Directions:

Sprinkle chili powder over crust's inside. Mix the cheeses with the flour and put them in the crust.   Mix the whites, milk, chilies, olives, salt and pepper together. Sprinkle cheese over it.   Bake for 45–55 minutes at 325°, or until a knife inserted in the middle comes out clean. Let it cool for 10 minutes, before the wedges are removed.   Nutrition: Calories: 550; Carbs: 40g; Fat: 35g; Protein: 20g

141. Denny Pancake Puppies

Preparation Time: 10 minutes Cooking Time: 5 minutes Servings: 6

Ingredients:

Vegetable oil, for frying   1/3 cup of milk   1 cup of Aunt Jemima Original Pancake Mix   1 egg   1 tablespoon of finely chopped white chocolate chips   1/2cup of chopped dried blueberries   Powdered sugar, for dusting

Directions:

In a deep fryer, preheat oil. Combine pancake mixture, milk, and egg into a medium bowl. Add the chocolate chips and blueberries and stir. Let the batter sit in to thicken for 10 minutes. Use an oil-coated ice cream scoop to make a batter ball, when the oil is hot, and drop it into the hot oil. Cook for 2½–3 minutes, until the batter is dark brown. Place on paper towels to drain and top with powdered sugar. Nutrition: Calories: 390; Fat: 12; Carbs: 67g; Protein: 6g

142.   Cheddar Honey Butter Croissants

Preparation Time: 40 minutes Cooking Time: 25 minutes Servings: 12

Ingredients:

Croissant Dough: 3 1/2 cup of all-purpose flour plus more to flour work surface 1 1/3 cup of milk 2 1/4 teaspoon of yeast (1 envelope) 1 1/2 teaspoon of salt 2 tablespoon of vegetable oil   1 tablespoon of granulated sugar 1 1/2 cup of butter cold, 3 sticks Egg Wash: 1 egg 1 teaspoon of heavy whipping cream Honey Butter Drizzle: 1/4 cup of unsalted butter 2 1/2 tablespoon of honey 3 tablespoon of powdered sugar

Directions:

For The Croissant Dough; Combine flour, milk, yeast, salt, vegetable oil, and sugar using a stand mixer with a dough hook. Mix the dough on low for 3 minutes. If you do not have a stand mixer, mix the ingredients together with a spoon until they begin to thicken, then kneed it with your hands. The dough is ready when it no longer is so sticky that it clings to your fingers or the dough hook. The dough should be tacky, but easy to detach and roll into a ball. Grease a large bowl with butter, and then place the croissant dough ball inside. Cover bowl with plastic wrap and allow dough to rise for 1-2 hours in a warm environment. Tip: I ran my dryer on low heat for 20 minutes, turned it off, and then placed the bowl inside with the door closed. While dough rises, cut each stick of cold butter lengthwise into 3 pieces. Place butter slices in a Ziploc bag (quart sized), arranging them in as close to a flat layer as possible. Using a rolling pin, roll and press the butter so that the edges fuse together and the butter reaches the edges of the bag. This will create a solid 8x8 square of butter. Cut butter out of Ziploc bag, and then wrap the butter square in plastic wrap. Place butter back in the refrigerator until dough is ready. Once the dough has risen, the next step is to "laminate" the dough, which is a special technique of folding the cold butter within the croissant dough. Once the dough has been laminated, refrigerate it overnight. Remove cold dough from refrigerator. Prepare 2 baking sheets by lining them with parchment paper. The dough must remain cold while working (to prevent butter within from melting), so before beginning, divide the dough in half. Keep one half to work with and place the other half in the refrigerator so that it remains cold until ready to be used. Generously flour your work space. Place the dough down and roll into a 7 x 20" rectangle, using more flour to prevent sticking as necessary. Cut triangles within the dough, making the small point about 1/4 inch wide and the wide end about 4–5 inches wide. Once cut, roll croissants starting from the wide base toward the small point. Place croissants on the baking sheet 2 inches apart. If desired, curl the ends of the croissant for a more decorative look. Remove the other half of the dough from the refrigerator and repeat the same steps. Prepare the egg wash by whisking together the egg and cream. Coat the croissants generously with the egg wash using a pastry brush. Allow the croissants to rise for another 1-3 hours at room temperature. The dough will puff slightly and should wiggle if the baking bowl is lightly shaken. Preheat the oven to 375°F. Bake the croissants for 25–35 minutes or until tops are golden brown. For The Honey Butter Drizzle: In a microwave safe bowl, heat butter until melted, about 45 seconds. Whisk in honey and powdered sugar. If the honey will not fully dissolve, heat the sauce for another 20 seconds. Putting It All Together: Serve the croissants warm with honey butter drizzled on top or as a dipping sauce on the side. Nutrition: Calories: 440; Fat: 30g; Carbs: 36g; Protein: 5g

143.   Panda Express Chicken Pot Stickers

Preparation Time: 40 minutes Cooking Time: 30 minutes Servings: 50

Ingredients:

1/2cup + 2 tablespoons of soy sauce, divided   1 tablespoon of rice vinegar   3 tablespoons of chives, divided   1 tablespoon of sesame seeds   1 teaspoon of sriracha hot sauce   1-pound of ground pork   3 garlic cloves, minced   1 egg, beaten - 11/2tablespoons of sesame oil   1 tablespoon of fresh ginger, minced   50 dumpling wrappers - 1 cup of vegetable oil, for frying   1/4of water

Directions:

In a mixing bowl, whisk together the 1/2cup of soy sauce, vinegar, and 1 tablespoon of the chives, sesame seeds and sriracha to make the dipping sauce.   In a separate bowl, mix together the pork, garlic, egg, the rest of the chives, the 2 tablespoons of soy sauce, sesame oil and the ginger.   Add 1 tablespoon of filling to each dumpling wrapper. Pinch the sides of the wrappers together to seal. You may need to wet the edges a bit, so they'll stick. Heat the cup of oil in a large skillet. When hot, working in batches, add the dumplings and cook until golden brown on all sides. Take care of not overloading your pan.   Add the water and cook until tender, then serve with the dipping sauce. Nutrition: Calories: 260; Fat: 6g; Carbs: 39g; Protein: 13g

144. Panda Express Chicken Egg Roll

Preparation Time: 10 minutes Cooking Time: 5 minutes Servings: 6-8

Ingredients:

2 tablespoons of soy sauce, divided 2 garlic cloves, minced, divided 2 green onions, chopped, divided 3 tablespoons of vegetable oil, divided 1/2 pound of boneless skinless chicken breasts, cooked whole & cut in pieces 1/2 head of green cabbage, thinly shredded 1 large carrot, peeled and shredded 1 cup of bean sprouts 12–16 egg roll wrappers 1 tablespoon of cornstarch mixed with 3 tablespoons water Peanut Oil for frying

Directions:

In a resalable plastic bag, combine 1 tablespoon of the soy sauce with 1 clove of minced garlic, 1 green onion, and 1 tablespoon of the oil. Mix well. Add the cut-up chicken pieces, seal the bag, and squish it around to make sure the chicken is covered. Refrigerate for at least 30 minutes. After the chicken has marinated, pour 1 tablespoon of the oil into a large skillet and heat over medium-high heat. When the oil is hot, add the chicken and cook, stirring occasionally, until the chicken is cooked through. Remove the chicken from the skillet and set aside. Pour the remaining tablespoon of oil into the skillet and add the cabbage, carrots and remaining soy sauce. Cook and stir until the carrots and cabbage start to soften, then add the bean sprouts and the remaining garlic and green onions. Cook another minute or so. Drain the chicken and vegetables thoroughly using either cheesecloth or a mesh strainer. Getting all the excess liquid out will keep the egg rolls from getting soggy. In a Dutch oven or large saucepan heat 3 inches of oil to 375°F. Place about 2 tablespoons of the chicken and vegetables into the center of each egg roll wrapper. Fold the ends up and roll up to cover the filling. Seal by dipping your finger in the water and cornstarch mixture and covering the edges. Cook the egg rolls in batches, a few at a time, for about five minutes or until golden brown and crispy. Remove from oil to a paper towel-lined plate to drain. Nutrition: Calories: 349; Fat: 4g; Carbs: 176g; Protein: 13 g

145. Starbucks Pink Drink

Preparation time: 5 minutes Cooking time: 0 minutes Servings: 2

Ingredients:

2 cups passion tea, brewed, cooled 1/2cup heavy cream 2 tablespoons vanilla syrup, sugar-free 1 1/2cup ice cubes

Directions:

Add all the ingredients in the order into a food processor except for ice, shut with the lid, and then pulse for 1 minute until smooth.   Divide the ice cubes evenly between two glasses, pour in the drink, and then serve. Nutrition: Calories 379 Fats 21 g Protein 2 g Net Carb 4 g Fiber 0 g

146. Starbucks Coffee Frappuccino

Preparation time: 5 minutes Cooking time: 0 minutes Servings: 2

Ingredients:

1/2cup heavy cream 1/2cup strong coffee, brewed, cooled 3/4 tablespoons erythritol sweetener 3 tablespoons caramel sauce, low-carb 1 1/2cups ice cubes 1/4 cup whipping cream

Directions:

Add all the ingredients in the order into a food processor except for whipping cream, shut with the lid, and then pulse for 1 minute until smooth.   Divide the drink evenly between two glasses, top with the whipped cream, and then serve. Nutrition: calories 182 Fats 14.7 g Protein 1 g Net Carb 0.5 g Fiber 0.6 g

147. Starbucks Vanilla Bean Frappuccino

Preparation time: 5 minutes Cooking time: 0 minutes   Servings: 2

Ingredients:

1/2cup heavy whipping cream 1 cups vanilla almond milk, unsweetened 1/2teaspoon liquid stevia, vanilla flavored 1/2of vanilla bean, split lengthwise, inside scraped out 1/2cup whipped cream 1 cup of ice cubes 2 teaspoons chocolate shavings, low-carb

Directions:

Add all the ingredients in the order into a food processor except for whipped cream, ice, and chocolate shavings, shut with the lid, and then pulse for 1 minute until smooth. Add ice and then continue blending for 30 seconds until the ice has crushed Divide the drink evenly between two glasses, top with the whipped cream, sprinkle with chocolate shavings, and then serve. Nutrition: Calories 217 Fats 23 g Protein 1 g Net Carb 2 g Fiber 0 g

148. Starbucks Egg Bites with Cheese and Red Pepper

Preparation time: 5 minutes Cooking time: 10 minutes   Servings: 3

Ingredients: 1/4cup chopped roasted red pepper 1 green onion, chopped 1/4cup chopped spinach 1/4teaspoon salt 1/4teaspoon ground black pepper 1/4teaspoon hot sauce 1/2cup cottage cheese 1 cup of water 4 eggs 1/2cup shredded Monterey jack cheese

Directions:

Crack eggs in a food processor, add salt, black pepper, and both cheese and pulse for 1 minute until smooth. Tip the mixture into a large bowl, add spinach, pepper, and onion and then stir until combined. Take three silicone cups or ramekins, pour in prepared batter evenly, and then cover each mold with foil. Switch on the instant pot, pour water into the inner pot, insert a trivet stand, and then place prepared ramekins on top. Cover the pot with lid, make sure it is sealed, press the steam button, and let it cook for 10 minutes. When the instant pot, press the cancel button, let the pressure release naturally for 10 minutes, and then do quick pressure release. Carefully open the instant pot, remove the ramekins from it, cool then for 5 minutes, and then uncover them. Transfer egg bites to a plate and then serve. Nutrition: Calories 286 Fats 19.7 g Protein 23.6 g Net Carb 3.2 g Fiber 0.4 g

149.   Starbucks Sous Vide Egg Bites

Preparation time: 5 minutes Cooking time: 8 minutes Servings: 4

Ingredients:

4 strips of bacon, cooked, chopped 1/2teaspoon salt 1/4teaspoon hot sauce 1/2cup cottage cheese 4 eggs 3/4 cup shredded mozzarella cheese 1/4cup heavy cream 1 cup of water

Directions:

Crack eggs in a food processor, add salt, hot sauce, cream, and both cheeses and pulse for 1 minute until smooth. Take four silicon molds, distribute chopped bacon in them, evenly pour in egg batter, and then cover each mold with foil. Switch on the instant pot, pour water into the inner pot, insert a trivet stand, and then place prepared ramekins on top. Cover the pot with lid, make sure it is sealed, press the steam button, and let it cook for 8 minutes. When the instant pot, press the cancel button, let the pressure release naturally for 10 minutes, and then do quick pressure release. Carefully open the instant pot, remove the ramekins from it, cool then for 5 minutes, and then uncover them. Transfer egg bites to a plate and then serve. Nutrition: Calories 258.8 Fats 19.6 g Protein 18.1 g Net Carb 2.6 g Fiber 0 g

150. McDonald's Pico Guacamole Burger

Preparation Time:10 minutes Cooking time: 10 minutes Servings: 10

Ingredients:

One 1/2lbs ground beef salt and pepper Four pieces of leaf lettuce Four sesame seed buns Four slices white cheddar cheese Pico de Gallo: Four plum tomatoes (seeded and diced) 1/2cup fresh cilantro (chopped) One small white onion (finely chopped) 2–3 jalapeño peppers (seeded and chopped) One tablespoon fresh lime juice salt (to taste) Guacamole: Three ripe avocados (peeled and pitted) The juice of 1 lime One teaspoon salt One teaspoon fresh garlic (minced) 1/2cup onion (diced) Three tablespoons fresh cilantro (chopped) One pinch cayenne pepper

Directions:

For Pico de Gallo: Mix tomatoes, onion, peppers and cilantro in a pot. Season with lime juice and salt. Blend well. Cover, and cool for 1 hour. For Guacamole: Mash the avocados in a medium pot. Squeeze the lime juice into or apply. Season with salt. Mix in the coriander, tomatoes, and garlic onion. Mix with cayenne pepper. Cool for 1 hour. Make the ground beef into four equal patties and season with salt and pepper on both sides. Place the patties over medium-high heat on a large skillet. Cook over medium-high heat, turning regularly until fully cooked (it has reached 160 degrees F. internally). Top each patty During the last few minutes of cooking with a slice of A white cheddar cheese. Cook before cheese melts. Place every patty onto the bottom half of a bun. Top with a piece of lettuce, some Pico de Gallo and some guacamole. Nutrition: Calories: 320 Fat: 13g Fiber: 7 Carbs: 15g Protein: 20g

151. McDonald's Shamrock Shake

Preparation Time: 10 minutes Cooking time: 0 minutes Servings: 6

Ingredients:

6 cups of vanilla ice cream (1.5-quart container) 1 1/2 cups of whole milk 1/8 tsp of green food coloring (approximately 10-15 drops of liquid food coloring) 3/4 tsp of pure mint extract For serving Whipped cream Green sanding or sparkling sugar Maraschino cherries

Directions:

To the big blender, add ice cream, milk, mint extract and food coloring. I did mine in batches, but if you've got a large, strong blender, you might do it all at once. Mix until smooth. Pour into glasses to drink. If wanted, top with the whipped cream, green sugar and raspberry. Nutrition: Calories: 466 Fat: 18g Fiber: 6 Carbs: 27g Protein: 28g

152. McDonalds Mc Nuggets

Preparation Time: 2 hours' minutes Cooking Time: 30 minutes Servings: 6

Ingredients:

2 cups all-purpose flour 2 teaspoons onion powder 1/4 teaspoon garlic powder 2 eggs 1 1/2cup water 2 1/2teaspoons salt 1/2 teaspoon black pepper 1 teaspoon MSG 6 chicken breast fillets, each cut into 6-7 bite-sized pieces vegetable oil, for frying

Directions:

In a bowl, beat eggs with water. Set aside. Mix onion powder, garlic powder, pepper, salt, msg, and flout in another bowl. Put the chicken cubes in a food processor and pulse until it is smooth in texture. Shape into small nuggets and freeze for around 15-20 minutes. Once done, take it from the chiller, then coat with the dry mixture, then coat with egg mixture, and lastly, coat again with the dry mixture. Repeat until all shaped chicken nuggets are coated well. Freeze again for an hour. If the freezing time is almost done, heat oil to 175c. Take the nuggets out from the freezer and deep fry until crispy and golden brown Serve hot with your favorite sauce. Nutrition: Calories: 440 Fat: 28g Fiber: 2 Carbs: 26g Protein: 24g

153. IHOP Tilapia Florentine

Preparation Time: 30 minutes Cooking Time: 20 minutes Servings: 4

Ingredients: 1 package (6 ounces) of fresh baby spinach 6 teaspoons of canola oil, divided 4 tilapia fillets (4 ounces each) 1 egg, lightly beaten 2 tablespoons of lime juice 2 teaspoons of garlic-herb seasoning blend 1/4 cup of grated Parmesan cheese 1/2 cup of part-skim ricotta cheese

Directions:

Cook the spinach in 4 teaspoons of oil until wilted in a large non-stick skillet; drain. In the meantime, put the tilapia in a fattened 13-in. x 9-in. baking platter. Drizzle with remaining lime juice and oil. Sprinkle with a blend to season. Combine the egg, ricotta cheese and spinach in a small bowl; spoon filets over. Sprinkle with Parmesan. Bake for 15-20 minutes at 375°.
Nutrition: Calories: 680; Fat: 43g; Carbs: 34g; Protein: 43g

154. Restaurant & Bakery® Croissant French Toast

Preparation Time: 15 minutes Cooking Time: 10 minutes Servings: 2

Ingredients: 1/2cup of sugar 1 tablespoon of all-purpose flour 2 cups of heavy whipping cream 4 egg yolks, beaten 2 scoops of vanilla ice cream 1 tablespoon of vanilla extract Berry Sauce: 2 cups of fresh cut raspberries 2 tablespoons of sugar French Toast: 3 eggs 4 croissants, split 2 tablespoons of butter

Directions: Take a large saucepan and add flour and sugar. Mix them together. Gradually, put in cream and continue mixing until it makes a smooth mixture. Place this pan over medium-high heat and stir until it thickens and starts to bubble. Reduce the pan's heat to low and stir for 2 minutes, then immediately remove it from the heat. Take another bowl and beat egg yolks in it. Slowly add a small amount of the hot cream mixture and meld it well. Return this egg-milk mixture to the saucepan and cook again with occasional stirring until it reaches 160°F. Remove it from the heat then add vanilla and ice cream. Cover this mixture with plastic wrap and allow it to cool. Prepare the berry sauce. Add sugar along with raspberries to a saucepan. Cook this mixture on a simmer for 3 minutes; then remove it from the heat. Dip the croissant in the whisked egg mixture and sear them in a griddles pan until golden brown on both the sides. Serve the croissants with a dollop of vanilla cream and berry sauce on top. Nutrition: Calories: 765; Fat: 32g; Carbs: 99g; Protein: 22g

155. IHOP Stuffed French Toast

Preparation Time: 5 minutes Cooking Time: 25 minutes Servings: 6

Ingredients:

1 loaf of French bread Splash of milk 4 eggs 2 tablespoons of butter Canned strawberry pie filling or fresh strawberries, for garnish 1 (24.2-ounce) tub of Philadelphia Ready to Eat Cheesecake Filling Whipped cream, for garnish

Directions:

Slice the bread into slices that are 1" thick. Beat the eggs with milk in a bowl. Dip slices of bread into the egg batter. Attach a few butter pats to a pan, and let it melt. Fry the bread on each side for 2–3 minutes, until they're slightly brown. Put several tablespoons of the cheesecake filling on one slide of toast. Top on another slice. Garnish with sliced strawberries or top with canned strawberry pie filling. Top with whipped cream. Nutrition: Calories: 850; Carbs: 120g; Fat: 34g; Protein: 15g

156. California Kitchen Pizza Italian Chopped Salad

Preparation Time: 30 minutes Cooking Time: 0 minutes Servings: 6

Ingredients: Mixed greens: 1 big head (4 cups; 285g) of romaine lettuce 1 can (15 oz.; 439g) of chickpeas (additionally called garbanzo grains), drained pipes and washed 1 pint (2 cups; 300g) of antique cherry tomatoes cut into quarters 1/2 cup (48g) of extremely thinly cut reddish onion 1 cup (4 oz.; 120g) of chopped salami 1/2 cup (80g) of chopped pork 1 cup (5oz, 140g) of fresh mozzarella gems, halved 1/3 cup (40g) of thinly sliced pepperoncini 10-12 sizable fresh basil leaves behind Dressing: 2 tablespoons of freshly pressed lemon extract 2 tablespoons of Dijon mustard 3 tablespoons of cabernet white vinegar 3 teaspoons of white colored sweets 1 teaspoon of dried oregano 1 teaspoon of dried out parsley 1 garlic clove(1/2 tsp lessened) 1/3 cup of olive oil Sodium and pepper

Directions:

Dressing: Place every one of the dressing ingredients in a wide-mouth container. Season with salt and pepper—I add 1/2 teaspoon salt, and 1/4 teaspoon pepper. Place the bottle cover, and quickly shake to blend. Place bottle in the refrigerator and outlet there until all set to dress the salad that was tossed. Lettuce: Wash and cut the lettuce. I like to reduce the salad into ribbons (wrap the items right into stogies and afterwards very finely slice) and after that halve the ribbons—thinner mixed greens parts allow additional surface for the dressing to stick to. Utilize a mixed greens rewriter to ensure the lettuce is 100% dry before including every other ingredient. Tossed Salad Ingredients: Add in the drained pipes and washed chickpeas, quartered cherry tomatoes, very finely cut reddish onion, thinly sliced salami, chopped ham, halved mozzarella gems, and very finely sliced pepperoncini. Chiffonade the basil pieces (find Note 2) and add those right into the tossed salad. Toss the mixed greens and adjust add-ins to personal desire. (The amounts noted are basic tips of how we like this chopped salad. The ideal component of creating this homemade is you can easily add added garnishes to individual preference!). Add Dressing: cut the dressing from the refrigerator and drink for recombination again. Just apply the dressing to the amount of salad you'll be immediately delighting in. The mixed greens do not fit effectively with dressing so keep it separate until it's ready to eat right away! Surplus dressing: you may not utilize all the dressing in this tossed salad (outfit to desire). Leftover dressing maintains to a week in the fridge. 17 Nutrition: Calories: 313; Carbs: 24g; Protein: 48g; Fat: 82g

157. Starbucks Bagels

Preparation time: 10 minutes Cooking time: 18 minutes Servings: 6

Ingredients:

For the Bagels: 2 cups almond flour1 teaspoon onion powder 1 teaspoon garlic powder 1 tablespoon baking powder 1 teaspoon Italian seasoning 3 cups shredded mozzarella cheese 3 eggs, divided 5 tablespoons cream cheese For the Topping: 2/3 tablespoon sea salt 2 teaspoons onion powder 2 teaspoons garlic powder 3/4 tablespoon poppy seeds 1 tablespoon sesame seeds

Directions:

Switch on the oven, then set it to 425 degrees F and let it preheat. Meanwhile, take a baking sheet, line it with parchment paper, and then set aside until required. Take a large bowl, place flour in it, add onion powder, garlic powder, Italian seasoning, and baking powder and then stir until well combined. Prepare the egg wash and for this, take a small bowl, crack an egg in it, whisk well, and then set aside.   Take a medium heatproof bowl, place cream cheese and mozzarella in it, microwave for 1 minute and 30 seconds, stir until mixed, continue microwaving for another minute and then stir until well combined. Take a separate large bowl, crack the remaining eggs in it, add flour mixture and then whisk well by using an electric beater until incorporated and the dough comes together. Divide the prepared dough evenly into six pieces, roll each piece into a ball, press a thumb or finger in its center and then shape it like a bagel. Repeat with the remaining pieces and arrange bagels onto the prepared baking sheet. Take a small bowl, place all the ingredients for the topping in it and then stir until mixed. Brush the prepared egg wash on top of each bagel, sprinkle with the prepared topping seasoning and then bake for 13 to 15 minutes until golden brown. Serve straight away. Nutrition: Calories 449 Fats 35.5 g Protein 27.8 g Net Carb 6 g Fiber 4 g

Lightning Source UK Ltd.
Milton Keynes UK
UKHW020643080621
385138UK00011B/714

HELL'S GOOD GUY

A catalogue record for this book is available from the British Library.

ISBN: 9781527283138

For anyone who has given me a lift from one location to another, for everyone who has consistently and effectively supported me and for anyone who has been disappointed or hurt by my actions.

'I'm perfectly sure we're going to be hearing more about Arran'

George Galloway – Politician, Broadcaster and Writer

'Arran is professional; everything is good'

Richard Blackwood – Actor, Broadcaster and Comedian

'I believe that Arran has a bright future and will accomplish anything that he puts his mind to'

Dawn Butler – Politician and Broadcaster

'Hell's Good Guy is clever, funny and an all-round masterpiece. An enticing read, great book!'

Spuddz – Comedian and Rapper

'Hell's Good Guy is such an interesting read and concept, it's worthy of becoming an animated movie!'

Outset Studio

'Hell's Good Guy is a fully loaded book containing existential topics that will make for good viewing. A theatrical adaptation should be on the horizon'

Wayne Joseph – Actor and Drama Teacher

Contents

Foreword – By Karina Fernandez

I really enjoyed teaching Arran and the rest of his cohort from Beginners to Advanced - it was really exciting to see them not only develop individually as performers, but also to see the way they grew as a group. The way they pushed each other to do their best work made the standard across the group incredibly high and it was no surprise to see that a number of them have continued to work together beyond the end of the courses. It was a great pleasure to read *Hell's Good Guy* and to know that Arran developed it and worked on it with such dedication. It's great to see Arran's sense of humour and philosophical inquiry coming out in such enjoyable and interesting ways in his writing. I can imagine actors and actresses performing *Hell's Good Guy*, and I hope it finds a wide audience sparking all the debate and discussion it merits.

Karina Fernandez – Actress and City Academy Tutor

###

Preface

Most Saturdays throughout the second half of 2019 saw me attending acting classes. Those classes started with me wanting to enjoy a new experience, but they quickly developed into something more. I intended to go into the new year building on what my classmates and I had learned. I spent the first eight weeks of the year writing for 20 minutes every day, with the text forming a play.

Before presenting the completed play to my former classmates: I asked my cousin, Ryan and an English teacher, Leah, to analytically read it and let me know their thoughts. Ryan and Leah are very different people, but I knew they would give me their honest opinions. I watched Ryan become animated whilst reading the play to himself, he said the play was great and that he wanted to tell people about it. Leah said the play was excellent and how she was glad she had made time to read it.

I presented the play to four of my former classmates and one actor; we started performing and discussing the play every Sunday and several months later Ryan joined us. The performances and critiquing of the play allowed me to contemplate ways to subtly improve it. The most important improvement was: where audiences cannot see the performance, the narrator's lines serve as commentary and where audiences can see the performance, the narrator's lines serve as instructions. However, I only polished off the play after attending script writing classes at the end of 2020.

Emanuel, a former classmate from the acting class, indirectly helped me with the costs of enrolling on to the script writing course. Two other former classmates from the acting class were just as helpful: Ayushi is the only person who has consistently performed the play with others and me (via Zoom, on the phone and in a studio) up until the point of me writing this; Anna, who helped progress the cover of this book to what it is now, has been almost as present. Ryan who was following on from his earlier contributions advised me to rename two chapters: Chapter five was originally titled Military Grade Weapons and Chapter six was originally titled Fence-Sitting.

A few friends of mine: Kim, Saadia and Tim were the closest I came to having editors. They gave the play its final readings before it entered the book stage. All three of them indicated that the play's flows and nuances are further validated with each repeated read.

Introduction

The play allows for different portrayals of characters and it enables the performer to connect with the character how they see fit. That being stated, characters will at times be played one of two ways or a mixture of two ways, line-by-line or chapter-by-chapter according to their defaults and the nature of the dialogue.

Some performers will portray Alex as ambiguous or contradictory. A stoic Gatekeeper may suit a few chapters and an ultra-authoritative Gatekeeper may suit other chapters. An assertive Ezra could be shouting at a wary Skylar or an emotional Skylar could be speaking to a slippery Ezra. Icky might take on a condescending tone after sounding insecure a few lines earlier. Voice acting the narrator's lines in a demonic or an angelic voice will create an extra dynamic complementing the other performances.

The play has specific stage positions: The Consultation Zone which is described as being in the east of the temple is located 'downstage centre' at the front of the stage. Ezra's position is two-thirds back from the front of the stage on the cusp of 'centre stage' and 'upstage centre'. Skylar's position is on Ezra's right-hand side and Icky's position is on Ezra's left-hand side. Standing diagonally at a 45-degree angle, the Gatekeeper's position is on the cusp of 'centre stage' and 'left stage'. Standing diagonally at a minus 45-degree angle, Alex's position is on the cusp of 'centre stage' and 'right stage'. The map below illustrates the performers' onstage positions.

Temple North

Temple
West

Temple

East

AUDIENCE

S E I

G

CONS ZONE

Temple South

Chapter 1 –
Four Possible Outcomes

Narrator: Bright lights start to shine, as Alex opens his eyes to find himself standing in the southern section of a temple. He is wearing a grey suit and red shirt. The Gatekeeper stands opposite him in the north and she is covered in a long white gown. She stares at Alex.

Gatekeeper: Alex Middleton, relax and do not panic. You are dead and in a structure called the Temple.

Alex: I'm not dead! (pause) Who are you? (pause) Where am I? (pause) How did I get here?

Gatekeeper: I am a Gatekeeper; a person capable of using 100% of my brain at all times. We are over 500 trillion miles from Earth and you travelled here via super-ultra-interactive five-dimensional yellow-tide technology.

Alex: Why do I feel so tired? I feel half asleep. (pause) Why can't I hear all of my thoughts?

Gatekeeper: Sleep and death are almost the same. As for your thoughts, they will shortly reach you.

Alex: I am not dead; I don't remember dying.

Gatekeeper: With the exception of Gatekeepers and the Reincarnated, nobody remembers their first or last 1,000 days on Earth.

Alex: Why am I here?

Gatekeeper: After living 1,001 days or more, when someone has died, he or she faces judgement. If that person's good deeds exceed their bad deeds, they go to Heaven. If that person's bad deeds exceed their good deeds, they go to Hell. In special circumstances, a person may go through Reincarnation. In highly unusual circumstances, a person may be put to Perpetual Sleep.

Alex: I refuse to believe that I am dead!

Gatekeeper: Denial is understandable; however, the quicker you accept the facts the better. Alex, your good deeds and bad deeds have not exceeded each other.

Alex: What does this mean?

Gatekeeper: It means on Earth you did exactly as much good as you did bad. It also means you are staying here until I determine where you go.

Alex: Heaven or Hell?

Gatekeeper: As previously stated, in a process like this, there are four possible outcomes; Heaven, Hell, Reincarnation and Perpetual Sleep.

Narrator: Skylar, Icky and Ezra enter the Temple from Alex's left. Skylar is dressed in a denim dress and denim hat; Icky is fitted in a fashionable yellow boiler suit and Ezra is clothed in green army fatigues. They take their positions in the west of the Temple.

Gatekeeper: Alex let me introduce you to Ms Skylar Erakat.

Skylar: Hi Alex, I hope you're well.

Gatekeeper: Ms Icky Downing.

Icky: Hello Alex.

Gatekeeper: Plus, Mr Ezra Goodwin-O'Fallon.

Ezra: Alex, Alex, Alex.

Alex: Why are these people here?

Gatekeeper: They are here to help the process.

Alex: So, they are not here to help me and they are not here to help you?

Gatekeeper: They are here to help the process and passionately promote specific outcomes. Whether they appear for, or against you, their biases are strictly to their preferred outcomes.

Alex: I don't fully understand. Why these people?

Gatekeeper: Because they have studied your life and they know as much about your life as you do. Can the three of you state and confirm your desired outcomes for Alex?

Skylar: Alex my goal is to get you to Heaven, 50% of your deeds have been good, which absolutely deserves rewarding.

Icky: Alex after the life you've had, I think it's time you take a rest. Perpetual Sleep is where you will find peace.

Ezra: Alex tune in to my logic, Heaven won't accept a man as bad as you and Hell won't accept a man as good as you. Reincarnation is what's best; let's see Earth again.

Alex: Now tell me, Gatekeeper, what do you want?

Gatekeeper: I want you to go to a deserved place.

Alex: Please cut the diplomacy; I know you don't like me.

Gatekeeper: That is projection Alex, projection. It is you who does not like me and trying to turn your issue, into my issue, will not help you advance.

Alex: Sorry, this is just difficult for me.

Gatekeeper: Before we start the process, do you have any questions?

Alex: Yes, firstly, thanks for the opportunity to prove myself and thanks for the brilliant way you have explained everything so far.

Gatekeeper: From one extreme to another. Treating someone you dislike in a friendly manner, to hide your true feelings is called reaction formation. (pause) Please just ask your question so we can start.

Alex: OK, how did I die? I need to know.

Gatekeeper: Unfortunately, I cannot tell you.

Alex: Hmm, you don't know.

Gatekeeper: I know all about you, everything from your birth to your death. However, I am prohibited from directly giving you such information, as per rules put in place before my ascension.

Alex: Can Skylar, Icky or Ezra tell me?

Gatekeeper: No, they only know as much about your life as you do.

Alex: I have a theory on how I may have died, as a goodwill gesture can you let me know if I at least have the right idea?

Gatekeeper: OK.

Alex: I used to put seeds in a trap to lure in red squirrels. Once I had the squirrels trapped, I would use them as live bait to lure in foxes. After having both the squirrels and foxes trapped, I would stop feeding the squirrels, let them die, gut them and stuff them ready for sale. I kept the foxes alive to use in a more elaborate game.

Skylar: That's not pleasant.

Icky: No, it's intelligent. I would imagine there's people in Hell who have done similar.

Ezra: It's a clever trap; it's perfect for outsmarting a simple-minded animal.

Gatekeeper: How does this connect to your theory?

Alex: I always thought karma would get me for my treatment of animals. I thought I would die in a similar trap at the hands of animals.

Gatekeeper: I can confirm that you do not have the right idea about your death. As for karma, it does not exist as an absolute science of what goes around comes around. In life there are only different types of actions.

Alex: OK.

Gatekeeper: Alexander, we are about to begin your afterlife trial. The discussion we will have, will allow me to determine whether you go into Heaven, into Hell, back to Earth via Reincarnation or are put to Perpetual Sleep. (pause) In the best interest of the process, we may all have one-to-one private conversations in the acoustically manipulated Consultation Zone. The transmission of a sound cancelling frequency means that nobody outside the Consultation Zone will hear what is said within it. The Consultation Zone is over there.

Narrator: The Gatekeeper points eastward towards the Consultation Zone.

Ezra: Gatekeeper, can I take an immediate consultation with Icky?

Gatekeeper: Go ahead.

Narrator: Ezra and Icky enter the Consultation Zone.

Icky: Why has one requested counsel so early? The trial hasn't even started.

Ezra: You said you want Alex put to Perpetual Sleep.

Icky: Yes, I did.

Ezra: You then mentioned people going to Hell for mistreating animals the way Alex did.

Icky: I did.

Ezra: Can you see the contradiction?

Icky: I admit it's a quandary; however, Perpetual Sleep is a good compromise, or maybe Alex should go somewhere else. (pause) Argh, I don't know.

Ezra: I don't think anyone's picked up on your indecision, but I could highlight that your confused indecisive state undermines the process and I could demand you be removed from the trial.

Icky: Why would you do that? Please don't do that.

Ezra: OK. Why don't you direct Alex's outcome towards Hell? With you passionately promoting Hell and Skylar promoting Heaven, the Gatekeeper is likely to choose an active outcome that sits in the middle – Reincarnation.

Icky: That's the outcome you want.

Ezra: Yes, I know what's best for Alex. I know what's best for Alex better than he does.

Icky: I should go outside and expose your corrupt proposition.

Ezra: You can if you want to, but as a consequence I will highlight your indecision. We would then both be removed from the process and we would never be taken seriously again. Now go out there and start promoting Hell, or otherwise, I'll make your existence hell!

Icky: Fine, I will.

Narrator: Ezra and Icky return to their positions and the trial begins.

Chapter 2 –
They All Hated Me

Gatekeeper: Alex, please tell us about the early part of your life.

Alex: Erm (pause) I was adopted at birth. I was brought up by a man who wasn't my father and I never had a mother.

Skylar: What were you told about your real parents?

Alex: I was told that my mother didn't want me and my father was unknown.

Icky: Did you endeavour to find your biological parents?

Alex: No.

Icky: Don't you think that's something you should have engaged in?

Alex: No, uniting with my birth parents was not my responsibility.

Skylar: Icky it could have been better to ask, whether his real parents tried to get in touch with him.

Ezra: I think questions about Alex's real parents are a waste of our time. Alex, what was your relationship like with your adoptive father?

Alex: If you know everything about my life that I do, why do you need to ask?

Ezra: I'm just here to help the process.

Gatekeeper: Alex, please answer the question.

Alex: No, why should I? You won't tell me how I died, so why should I answer anything?

Gatekeeper: Alex, by you asking questions at this time, you distance us from the question Ezra has asked. I appreciate that we are talking about your childhood; however, this doesn't mean you have to respond like a child.

Alex: Do you see a man or a child standing here?

Gatekeeper: I see a man here, a man clearly in regression.

Alex: Regression?

Gatekeeper: Regression, the process of reverting to a previous behaviour in your development. (pause) Ezra, please re-ask your question and Alex, please answer it.

Ezra: What was your relationship like with your adoptive father?

Alex: It was horrible (pause) horrific (pause) um, just horrible. I (pause) I found it a horrible relationship.

Icky: (speaking quickly) I'm sure it was a horrible horrifying horrific horror full of horrifically horrifying horribleness with horridness and other horribleness's that horrified (speaking with frustration) but can you please elaborate?

Alex: My adoptive father was both mentally and physically abusive. He was responsible for ruining my childhood. My adoptive father would be waiting for me to make a mistake, just so he could abuse me.

Skylar: Can you tell us about the mental abuse?

Alex: I was called names; I was often called Satan or Demon.

Icky: What did you experience in the way of physical abuse?

Alex: I would be laid flat on a bed and beaten with a cane on the soles of my feet.

Ezra: How else did your adoptive father ruin your childhood?

Alex: I used to play football with a neighbour and his sons in the back garden. When I was around the age of nine, the neighbour took me to join a Sunday league team. I played in goal for two seasons. Yours truly was the man of the match nearly every game; I won awards and I made friends with good people. I actually felt like I had a family.

Ezra: That doesn't sound bad, but please carry on.

Alex: My adoptive father didn't watch me once, but his brother, the Bishop, used to watch me play football and then afterwards take me to Sunday worship. Two years into playing Sunday league football, two professional football clubs wrote to my adoptive father inviting me to a trial with their youth teams. My adoptive father responded by banning me from playing football or speaking to my football family, including our neighbours and his sons.

Skylar: That must have felt awful.

Icky: How did your adoptive father justify that decision?

Alex: He didn't. He simply said that football was getting in the way of our faith and imposed his ban. He didn't understand that football was my religion and my escape from his abuse. The only positive was that my adoptive uncle, the Bishop, understood how I felt.

Icky: I'm starting to see how horrific things were; on the other hand, you were horrible too.

Alex: I was no Angel, but what do you mean?

Icky: Your adoptive father was tasked by his brother, the Bishop, with looking after the church's finances. He outsourced that responsibility to you, but you at the age of 11, decided to steal and hide £20 a week.

Alex: Yes, I did, it was for my survival and liberation fund. I had decided that at the age of 16, I would get away from my adoptive father and all the madness that came with him.

Icky: Do you not think that stealing from the congregation was wrong?

Ezra: It was about survival and liberation.

Alex: Yes, it wasn't about right and wrong; survival and liberation was the motive.

Skylar: Didn't you fear the consequences of someone finding out?

Alex: No, I couldn't imagine I would suffer any more than I already had. Look, when I was removed from the football team a part of me died, I've never been the same since then.

Skylar: In general, how did you cope? What did you do to release your anger?

Alex: I would fight with my adoptive cousins. I would beat the hell out of them.

Icky: Just the females. Why didn't you fight with your adoptive father and others?

Alex: You're making it sound a lot more sinister than it was. My adoptive cousins were older than me and I would always challenge my adoptive cousins to a fight, not just attack them.

Icky: Why didn't you challenge your adoptive father to a fight?

Ezra: Alex wasn't even a teenager; there was no way he was going to beat a grown man in a fight.

Gatekeeper: OK, I want to progress. Two things were going on, one of them being displacement. Displacement is where you take out impulses on a less threatening target, which is what Alex was doing by fighting with his adoptive cousins instead of his adoptive father. Does everyone understand?

Ezra: Yes.

Skylar: Yeah.

Icky: Yes, certainly.

Gatekeeper: The other thing that was taking place was sublimation. Sublimation is where you make something traditionally seen as wrong, acceptable in a social or formal setting.

Icky: Are you still referring to Alex fighting with his adoptive cousins?

Gatekeeper: Yes.

Skylar: Why did Alex only challenge older females?

Gatekeeper: Well, his mother was not there to protect him, so, he transferred his anger.

Alex: Can we please keep this process moving?

Gatekeeper: Alright. Alex, tell us, what was your relationship like with your wider adoptive family?

Alex: Except for my adoptive uncle, the Bishop, I hated my adoptive family as much I hated my adoptive father. They were generally a clueless bunch and offered me nothing of value. I had nothing in common with them, I just played a game of staying civil until I could be free of them. In basic terms they all loved each other, my adoptive father loved them and hated me. In fact they all hated me.

Gatekeeper: Alex, with everything going on, how was schooling and general education affected?

Skylar: Gatekeeper, sorry to interrupt, but can we please have a consultation?

Gatekeeper: Yes.

Narrator: Skylar and the Gatekeeper enter the Consultation Zone.

Skylar: Gatekeeper, I appreciate I am not here to tell you what to do and I am not trying to do that now.

Gatekeeper: Alright.

Skylar: I think we all should have already examined Alex's feelings about his mother, or at least talk about them now, as we haven't explored them.

Gatekeeper: Well, factoring in your preferred outcome and your contribution so far, it seems you are almost playing the role of Alex's mother, so I don't think it is necessary. Is there anything else?

Skylar: No.

Narrator: Skylar and the Gatekeeper return to their positions.

Gatekeeper: Right, Alex, how was your schooling and general education affected?

Alex: Once I finished year six and my fun playing football was over; I was put into a church-controlled school, which was next to my adoptive uncle's church and opposite the church's cemetery.

Icky: Maybe that's what you needed and perhaps where you should have stayed.

Skylar: Well, it may not have been what you wanted, but in the short-term it at least gave you something else to focus on.

Alex: No, I don't see it that way. It was horrendous; it was the last thing I needed. I was at school Monday to Friday, nine until four. I had Saturday school to attend and two church services on Sunday, two evenings a week I had Bible studies and the rest of the time was filled with homework.

Ezra: An escape is what was needed.

Alex: The escape came at 16. I took all the savings from the church money I had stolen and I travelled to a faraway city. I rented a room above a slaughterhouse and I started reading non-religious books and followed things that interested me.

Skylar: How did you feel leaving your life behind?

Alex: I felt happy leaving my life behind. My money, my passport and the Bishop's phone number were all that I took with me. I decided to only keep in touch with my adoptive uncle and I started referring to him as just, Bishop, that way I didn't have to associate him with my adopted family.

Icky: Gatekeeper, I sense we're concluding the discussion around Alex's formative and schooling years. Before we do so, can you indulge me with your presence in the Consultation Zone?

Gatekeeper: Certainly.

Narrator: Icky and the Gatekeeper enter the Consultation Zone. Skylar sees Ezra making nervy facial expressions whilst he looks at the Consultation Zone.

Icky: Gatekeeper, in responding to our questions, Alex is playing the victim.

Gatekeeper: He is answering the questions from his point of view and that is expected.

Icky: For the remainder of the process, one urges you to probe Alex a lot deeper.

Gatekeeper: Thank you for the suggestion; however, I will manage this whole process as I see fit, the discussion included.

Icky: Of course.

Gatekeeper: I suggest that you focus on your own contribution towards the process.

Icky: Gatekeeper, when we return to the trial, one would like to ask a few further questions about what has been discussed up to this point.

Gatekeeper: You can ask one or two questions and then we will move on.

Narrator: Icky and the Gatekeeper return to their positions. Skylar notices that Ezra still looks nervous.

Icky: Alex I have two final questions regarding your childhood.

Ezra: I hope your questions are aligned with your preferred outcome.

Skylar: Or aligned with the best outcome.

Gatekeeper: Icky, ask your questions.

Icky: Why didn't you report your adoptive father's abusive behaviour?

Alex: I was too afraid that nobody would believe me. My adoptive father was a master of pretending to be a nice person, in fact he was a nice person to everyone but me.

Icky: Indeed. (pause) In your opinion is purloining money from the church, the type of deed that warrants a place in Heaven or a place in Hell?

Alex: Good gosh. (pause) It warrants a place in Hell.

Skylar: Icky remember the circumstances; Alex was in distress at that time.

Icky: Whether you factor in his miserable childhood or not, he has said it himself, purloining from the church warrants a place in Hell.

Skylar: A man that is 50% good, cannot go to Hell.

Ezra: I think we can rule out Heaven or Hell.

Gatekeeper: I will be the judge of that. (pause) Alex, you travelled to a faraway city and started renting a room. What happened next?

Chapter 3 –
666 Miles

Alex: After traveling 666 miles and renting a room, I gained employment at the slaughterhouse. I watched and learned; I asked questions and tried to progress.

Gatekeeper: What did progression look like?

Alex: I started earning a lot of money doing work off the books.

Skylar: What did 'off the books' entail?

Alex: It involved setting traps for novelty creatures, killing them, stuffing them and selling them on the black-market to associates in the criminal underworld.

Gatekeeper: What did you stuff inside the creatures?

Alex: Every illegal item you can imagine.

Skylar: That's not good Alex.

Ezra: Alex did what he had to do to increase his income.

Icky: It's ruthless and deceptive, yet income augmentation is income augmentation.

Gatekeeper: Alex, would you have killed people for money?

Alex: No!

Gatekeeper: Icky, do you think Alex would have killed people for money?

Icky: If the money was right, he would have killed people and disposed of the bodies at the abattoir.

Gatekeeper: Ezra, what do you think?

Ezra: I would rather not answer a hypothetical question about murder, but when someone is desperate anything is possible.

Skylar: The fact is Alex has never killed a human, even when under pressure Alex never resorted to that.

Alex: Exactly. Whether my choices were right or wrong, my goal was to make a life for myself. Unfortunately, making a life for myself meant long hours preying on animals and committing to other risky tasks in the criminal underworld.

Gatekeeper: What did you do in your free time?

Alex: I enjoyed my freedom; I started doing things that a 16-year-old does.

Gatekeeper: Such as?

Alex: This and that.

Ezra: You started reading rare books, listening to independent music and you played a season of football.

Icky: One of those books was called 'The Oath of Unlucky Number 13', you listened to the song 'More Murder' twice a day and you broke someone's leg playing football.

Skylar: One of the books was called 'The Jovial Relationship between Malcolm and Martin', he listened to the song 'Private Prayer' more than twice a day and breaking his teammate's leg was an accident.

Icky: You lost your virginity in the new city. Let's talk about that in detail.

Alex: No, no, no!

Icky: She was a horny woman, old enough to be your mother.

Alex: We are not talking about that.

Ezra: Maybe we should talk about that; Alex if you don't, I will.

Alex: Keep your mouth shut!

Skylar: You're overreacting.

Alex: I'm not!

Skylar: Yes, you are.

Alex: No, I am not!

Skylar: You're overreacting to avoid the topic.

Alex: You know nothing about my reactions!

Skylar: (speaking quickly) I know that your abstractional overreaction is the actionable reaction that you hope will start a chain-reaction creating coaction which will be a unique factional distraction from the original counteraction ultimately inviting dissatisfaction and protraction in this process (speaking with frustration) which sees us not talking about your sex life.

Gatekeeper: Alex, please summarise your sex life.

Alex: I had a brief casual relationship with a woman named Jazzy and many years later I had sex with a prostitute.

Gatekeeper: How did the brief casual relationship start?

Alex: I passed my driving test and bought a used car that I had seen advertised. I had to give the former owner, Jazzy, a lift back home as part of the deal. On arrival at her place, she invited me in.

Icky: Quick work.

Ezra: Smooth operator.

Alex: We did it that night and again the next night in the car. We went at it so aggressively we ended up damaging the car and I eventually had to get it fixed. Jazzy and I had sex on one more occasion, but before climaxing we were interrupted by her business partner Anisha.

Gatekeeper: How did this entire explicit episode finish?

Alex: A day later Jazzy explained that sex with me was just rebound sex. She said it had to stop as she had feelings for someone else. In time I discovered I knew who that person was and I also discovered I knew one of his friends. I was ambivalent about the decision at first, but in hindsight I was glad Jazzy had ended our explicit episodes before it got messy.

Icky: Why would it have got messy?

Alex: At different times several years later, Jazzy's love interest, Mani and his friend, Sam, helped me progress my career. If I had stayed involved with her, I would have mixed business with pleasure. I also found Anisha more attractive than Jazzy and if I had stayed involved with Jazzy thinking like that, I would have endured mixed feelings and turmoil.

Ezra: You could have juggled all of that.

Alex: No chance! From my perspective Jazzy, Anisha, Sam and Mani were a tricky bunch, but that's probably a story for another day.

Skylar: A woman like that doesn't suit you.

Alex: I agree, a woman like Jazzy doesn't suit me but it was one heck of an experience.

Icky: It felt great relieving all those sinful urges, didn't it?

Alex: Erm, no comment.

Gatekeeper: Did you use a condom?

Alex: I have no further comments to make on this.

Ezra: We all know the answer anyway.

Skylar: Now could be a good time to talk about Vasia?

Gatekeeper: Yes, now would be a good time to talk about her.

Chapter 4 –
A Saviour

Alex: I had recently turned 20 and had been driving for three months. I was picking up my car from the mechanics; the mechanic was behind schedule and my car wasn't going to be ready for an hour. I decided to wait in the reception area where I met a 24-year-old Vasia. She was conscientiously manning the reception desk.

Icky: First impressions?

Alex: She was alluring, especially for a mechanic's receptionist. We had a conversation, a conversation I cannot remember. As you all know everything about my life that I do, maybe one of you can remind me?

Skylar: There was something on the radio about child abuse and the two of you ended up talking about that for 55 minutes. You both talked with such passion and awareness.

Icky: You made a great first impression; Vasia was impressed with your understanding and articulation of the topic. The two of you conversed with remarkable chemistry.

Alex: Why can't I remember that the way the both of you do?

Ezra: Maybe we can save the subject of Vasia for another time, in another life maybe.

Gatekeeper: Alex, suppression is the act of stopping yourself from thinking or feeling something.

Alex: Well, things not working out with Vasia is one of my biggest regrets. I've never been able to talk about the relationship since it ended, but I didn't realise that extended to my thinking.

Gatekeeper: The suppression of Vasia associated memories was a war you fought out in your conscious mind and the suppression then extended to your verbal expression.

Alex: I do not have wars in my mind.

Skylar: You do.

Ezra: Yes, you do.

Icky: We all do.

Gatekeeper: Alex, what does t, h, o, u, g, h, t spell?

Alex: Thought.

Gatekeeper: What does f, o, u, g, h, t spell?

Alex: Fought. Oh, I see.

Gatekeeper: Whether it be one man or groups of people, thinking and fighting are usually one and the same. Even creating a fort, f, o, r, t, around Vasia associated memories is a part of the same process. Now please continue talking about Vasia.

Alex: I left with my car and a few days later Vasia called me. She explained that she knew it was unprofessional to call a customer for personal reasons, but she had liked speaking with me and wondered if we could meet for a coffee. I said: 'yeah, sure.'

Skylar: What were you expecting that coffee to lead to?

Ezra: Rumpy pumpy, break the bed.

Alex: Oh no, I was just happy to meet and have a coffee. I thought it would be over in 20 minutes, but we ended up staying out for 14 hours.

Icky: That was a splendid day.

Alex: Yeah, we had coffee, talked for hours, watched a movie, devoured dinner at a vegan restaurant and then drank soft drinks at a bar. I loved being with her; after that date I was totally hooked.

Skylar: What did Vasia see in you?

Alex: I don't know; we just seemed to click. Our energy and chemistry mixed like a dream.

Icky: You said you loved being with her. The two of you became an item after five dates. Did you have any negative feelings?

Alex: I feared meeting her family as her boyfriend.

Ezra: Why?

Alex: Because, they were Muslims and I was raised in the church. I had opened my mind through reading, but I was unsure of my religion. I just didn't want to meet her family and come off as confused.

Skylar: How did you get on with her family?

Alex: I went to the mosque, not to meet her family, but to learn about Islam. Nevertheless, I met her mum, dad and two brothers, they saw us as close friends, rather than two people in a relationship. Except for kissing, there was no sexual aspect to our relationship, so even in my mind it felt like an extra special friendship. Vasia's dad loved having me around and in the early stages of the relationship he even offered me a job. I turned the job offer down as at that time I had steady employment.

Skylar: What positives did Vasia bring to your life?

Alex: New experiences and a new way of living. I got to see a family environment and I got to be a part of a loving family dynamic. I stopped swearing and I haven't sworn since. I went on holidays and I started eating better. Most importantly, I was largely inactive in the criminal underworld.

Skylar: Vasia was exactly what you needed; she was like a saviour who reinvigorated you.

Alex: You took the words right out of my mouth.

Icky: So, why did you mess up the romance of the century?

Alex: Sex before marriage was a big issue for Vasia; I had spent over four years with her and that was a long time to go without sex. Regrettably, I cheated on her with a prostitute.

Icky: Well, we've all got needs.

Skylar: Icky that's not good enough. Putting the sex aside why didn't you ask Vasia to marry you?

Alex: I just wasn't ready to get married.

Ezra: You didn't need to marry her.

Alex: I think (pause) maybe I should have; I was just scared and sexually frustrated.

Gatekeeper: How did it end for you and Vasia?

Alex: Not good.

Gatekeeper: Elaborate.

Alex: I told someone, who told someone, who told someone about my episode with the prostitute and it got back to Vasia. She left me and married someone else less than six months later.

Icky: Who did you tell about you cheating?

Alex: I can't remember.

Skylar: You should think about it.

Ezra: Alex can't remember who that someone was so let's move on.

Alex: I told some obscure person, who told someone, who told someone, who told Vasia, but the obscure person shouldn't have said anything.

Icky: Who was that obscure someone?

Alex: I genuinely can't remember.

Ezra: (speaking quickly) Look, Alex should have told no one but someone told another someone who was happy to tell anyone allowing some other one to tell some anyone before telling another other one and then another anyone (speaking with frustration) Vasia found out and it was then all over.

Gatekeeper: Alex, as Ezra has implied you told a neighbour and things spread from there.

Alex: Sounds logical, but I don't think about these things (pause) although I do remember using a condom during that particular episode.

Skylar: Gatekeeper, can Alex and I have a consultation?

Gatekeeper: Yes, we will move on once you come out of the Consultation Zone.

Narrator: Skylar and Alex enter the Consultation Zone.

Skylar: Alex, I just wanted to give you a space to let your emotions out.

Alex: I'm fine.

Skylar: Really?

Alex: No. I loved her and I never once told her.

Skylar: I'm sure Vasia knew you loved her.

Alex: I regret cheating on her more than anything. I would go through every bad experience I ever had all over again if it meant getting 10 minutes with Vasia.

Skylar: What would you say?

Alex: I would gaze into her eyes and tell her I love her.

Skylar: Wow.

Alex: I still can't believe she moved on straight away.

Skylar: Why do you say that?

Alex: She married someone else less than six months after we broke up. Romantically, I never moved on or got over her; from time to time after dreaming about her, I would wake up with tears in my eyes.

Skylar: Do you think she married on the rebound?

Alex: I don't know. Vasia once said she would die before breaking up with me, I made one mistake and that statement became meaningless. Vasia getting married devastated me. I remember constantly texting the Bishop and him helping me navigate the turmoil.

Skylar: You showed strength in carrying on.

Alex: Yeah, I think so. (pause) I sincerely appreciate this, but we should go back to the trial.

Skylar: OK.

Narrator: Skylar and Alex return to their positions. Alex composes himself.

Alex: I want to have a further word on Vasia. She was flawless, well maybe she had one minor flaw.

Icky: What was that minor flaw?

Alex: She would buy me clothes I didn't need, with money she didn't really have, from shops I didn't like, to impress people I didn't care about. Other than that minor flaw, Vasia was perfect. I messed up the relationship, but her impact on me made me a better person.

Ezra: How so?

Alex: Shortly after our relationship ended, I never disrespected a woman again. I left the slaughterhouse and became a vegetarian; I started giving money to animal charities and I continued studying Islam.

Ezra: You could have done all that without her.

Alex: I don't think I would have.

Icky: You did all of that because you felt guilty and that was your way of atoning.

Alex: Possibly, but I still did the right thing.

Skylar: Good Alex, good.

Gatekeeper: After leaving the slaughterhouse what did you do for money?

Chapter 5 –
War Ready

Alex: Through Sam Fouler, a friend in the criminal underworld, I got a legitimate job managing a storage company.

Gatekeeper: Tell us about it.

Alex: I started working for William Seaman, he owned numerous businesses and employed me to work at his storage company.

Ezra: What was it like working for Willy Seaman?

Alex: It was hell. (pause) We worked long hours and were never paid overtime. Minimum wage is what we earned and our pay only increased when minimum wage increased.

Skylar: Did you ever complain?

Alex: We were bullied at work, but complaining about anything led to victimisation.

Icky: Nonetheless, did you personally complain?

Alex: No, it wasn't worth the stress. I had other ways of dealing with things.

Gatekeeper: Such as?

Alex: Over a two-year period, I studied the business and the storage industry. I would anonymously visit the local competitors and spy on them. I saw that their employees received the same treatment as we did. I constructed a plan.

Icky: Here it comes, the evil genius at work.

Alex: Actually, my plan was to improve the lives of all those who deserved better.

Skylar: What was the plan?

Alex: The plan was to rent 100,000 square feet of land and have 991 storage units built. There would be space for a gym and a vegan restaurant. The novelty was that both the gym and restaurant would be built out of large storage units.

Ezra: That was brave. Where did the money come from?

Alex: I phoned the Bishop and told him of that part of the plan. He agreed to lend me the money, which was to be paid back when I could afford to pay it back. The Bishop believed he was lending me enough money to rent the land for two years. In actuality, he was lending me enough money to rent the land for eight months and rent two vans, as well as complete the construction.

Skylar: Didn't you feel the plan was a bit risky?

Alex: No, I had planned night and day for two years. The key was to make sure the business started generating big money straight away. I planned to fill the facility in a few days of it opening.

Icky: That was all very audacious. How did you guarantee it would work?

Alex: I bribed two of the rival companies' managers. I paid for their customers' personal data, as well as electronic copies of their company headed paper. Before resigning, I took similar customer details from my employer.

Ezra: I'm getting goose bumps thinking about it all.

Alex: With the information I had, I paid for the construction of 200 one hundred square foot units, 101 two hundred square foot units, 300 fifty square foot units, 300 twenty-five square foot units and another 90 units of various sizes between 10 and 800 square feet.

Icky: Superbly calculated. How did you guarantee you would fill the space?

Alex: With the help of Lenny Jackson. Lenny Jackson was a criminal underworld connection; through his organisation I had a rival company's reception set on fire and another rival saw multiple storage units vandalised.

Skylar: That was not the way to do things.

Icky: If it worked, it worked.

Alex: The only downside was as payment for their services, I had to unofficially give 10% of all profits to Lenny Jackson's underworld organisation.

Ezra: I understand you damaged your competitors, but how exactly did you get the competitors' customers to come over to you?

Alex: I wrote them letters posing as their current storage provider. I apologised for the recent inconveniences and admitted to other serious problems. Those serious problems were fictitious.

Icky: Smart.

Skylar: No, it's highly dangerous.

Ezra: It's ballsy. Dangerous and smart.

Alex: Wait for it. I delivered leaflets through the doors of all the competitors' customers. The leaflets promoted my facility being staffed 24 hours a day, 365 days a year inclusive of security. I offered cheaper storage at my facility and customers had access to a free gym and a vegan restaurant. Eighty-five percent occupancy was enough to cover all costs. I was 89% occupied in nine days, the customers had come flocking in.

Ezra: That's thrilling. Two years on from leaving the slaughterhouse you owned a business and it was bringing in serious money. You did great.

Alex: Great, but not that great. I didn't have a house; I still rented a room and I sold my car back to Jazzy to help finance the business. Although I made a small profit, I knew that Lenny Jackson's organisation would want their cut to look healthy.

Icky: How much did you pay them?

Alex: After three months I had covered all costs and made a profit of £1,238. Lenny Jackson's organisation was due £124. I decided to give them all the profits.

Ezra: Why?

Alex: The £124 would have been an insult. I was actually told the full £1,238 was not enough and the 10% after other business-related favours would now be £2,000 a month. What's more, Lenny Jackson said I had to film a promotional video for the company website. I didn't think the video was a bad idea, but I didn't like being given the instruction.

Ezra: Damn right you didn't.

Gatekeeper: So, they were slowly going to take over your business?

Alex: Yes, they were going to bring hell to my corner.

Icky: Instinctively you always knew that would happen though?

Alex: I suppose.

Skylar: Oh dear, what did you do?

Alex: I had a sit-down with Lenny Jackson's people and asked how much it would cost to be rid of them for good.

Skylar: You actually believe you spoke to members of the criminal underworld like that?

Alex: No, I actually said: 'how much would it cost to buyout the 10%?'

Icky: What was the response?

Alex: They said I could have the 10% back for free, but the next storage company reception set on fire would be mine, with me in it, after my body had been opened up like a door.

Skylar: At that point, common sense says you would have backed down.

Ezra: No not our Alex.

Alex: I thanked them for returning my 10% and walked out.

Icky: Didn't you fear for your life?

Alex: Yes, I did, but I was never going to have Lenny Jackson take over my business. It would have been like selling my soul to the Devil. Anyhow, I knew from my time trapping and selling novelty creatures, that the only way to defeat a dangerous animal was to become more dangerous than that animal.

Icky: What did that entail?

Alex: I bought eight military grade weapons from a well-connected member of the criminal underworld, Mani Anderson. I told Mani to deliver the weapons to a specific storage unit at my facility.

Skylar: Why military grade?

Alex: I knew it would be hard for Mani to source a military grade weapon and he would have to talk to others. Word would naturally get back to Lenny Jackson that I was buying eight of them. Lenny Jackson would interpret that as me preparing for war.

Icky: Good you got yourself war ready.

Ezra: Yeah.

Skylar: That's all crazy.

Alex: No, it's not crazy. It's what I had to do to survive. When Mani delivered the weapons, he asked who was going to be using them? I knew he was really asking for Lenny Jackson. I told him I had ex-police men and ex-military on my payroll, he looked at me like I was nuts and told me to lose his contact details.

Icky: Weren't you running the risk of escalating the matter?

Alex: Things had already escalated, I was in the process of scaring them off, but I still needed something else to be sure. I approached the police; I arranged a meeting with a police inspector. I mentioned the recent criminality at the storage companies, then I asked if they could make themselves available to secure my facility.

Skylar: Alex you were the cause of the trouble at the storage companies.

Alex: I didn't tell the police inspector that.

Skylar: I'm sure you didn't, but confession is good for the soul.

Icky: I disagree. Confession is an expedited passage to prison.

Ezra: What did the police say?

Alex: They said no, but mentioned a well-known former police chief's security company. I already had security for my facility, but I still saw how it could work.

Ezra: How?

Alex: I hired the security company for a one-off occasion. I asked them to appear in the promotional video for my storage facility and generally secure the video shoot.

Icky: Bravo Alex. An idea that came from Lenny Jackson was ultimately used against him.

Alex: Yep. The criminal underworld all knew who the significant police figures were. Now with the false reality spreading that I had militarised police on my payroll, there was no way Lenny Jackson was going to come after me. It also meant I was fully finished with the underworld.

Icky: Gatekeeper, can Alex and I have a brief consultation?

Gatekeeper: Yes.

Narrator: Icky and Alex enter the Consultation Zone. Skylar notices that Ezra appears anxious.

Icky: In the face of indignity, one thought it was unequivocally brilliant how in a heightened situation, one managed to get on top and then stay in that position.

Alex: Thanks.

Icky: Although, I have never understood why you didn't kill Lenny Jackson. That would have made a great statement.

Alex: Killing people wasn't me.

Icky: Maybe one wasn't pushed hard enough. Why did one keep the rifles after the situation had attenuated?

Alex: I suppose I just forgot about them.

Icky: You can't keep playing the innocent. Nobody forgets about rifles; those rifles were always occupying the darkest regions of your mind.

Alex: I do remember deciding not to buy any bullets for those military grade weapons. I would never have used the bullets.

Icky: Never say never as everything has it's time and place.

Narrator: Icky and Alex return to their positions.

Alex: For those of you that want to plant the seed of me playing the victim or being some type of secret villain, I just want to say that I took multiple people out of minimum wage jobs and I paid them double minimum wage. I provided them with healthy meals for free, a gym for free and flexible working. Whilst doing that I worked 13 punishing hours every day for three hard years and because I paid myself less than the cleaners I lived in a room at someone else's house.

Icky: No rest for the wicked.

Alex: I wasn't wicked; my ventures were good.

Gatekeeper: If you were doing such good, why did you not keep it going?

Alex: I was burnt out. The freeholder made a great offer to buy the business. I was able to repay the Bishop with interest and donate to the church. The donation also covered all the money I stole in my youth. After all of that, I had enough money to travel back to my hometown and buy a property with a 66.6% deposit.

Ezra: In the end you only cared about yourself.

Alex: I don't see it that way.

Gatekeeper: Why did you travel back to your hometown and why did you purchase a property on the same street as the church?

Skylar: Yes, especially as you fled your childhood and preferred attending mosques.

Alex: It just felt like the right thing to do.

Ezra: Admit it, returning home after 14 years was about showing everyone how well you had done.

Alex: Partly, but I felt I had to go home.

Gatekeeper: OK, Alex, thank you. (pause) Alex, what are your religious views?

Chapter 6 –
Great Doesn't Mean Good

Alex: I have studied the Bible and the Quran, Christianity and Islam. I don't have a specific view.

Gatekeeper: Would you say one religion is superior to the other?

Alex: I don't have a specific view.

Gatekeeper: Should I assume you see both religions as equal?

Alex: The Quran says: 'O you who have believed, avoid much assumption. Indeed, some assumption is sin.' The Bible says: 'Let us stop passing judgment on one another.'

Gatekeeper: Alex, please stop sitting on the fence.

Ezra: Gatekeeper, maybe Alex sees both religions as insignificant as each other, I know I do.

Alex: I do not have a specific view!

Gatekeeper: Alex, what does Christmas mean to you?

Alex: It's the time of the year where I see people get more drunk than usual. Additionally, the Bible says: 'Learn not the way of the heathen and be not dismayed at the signs of the heathen; for the heathen are dismayed at them. For the customs of the people are vain, for one cutteth a tree out of the forest, the work of the hands of the workman with the axe. They deck it with silver and with gold; they fasten it with nails and with hammers, that it moves not.'

Gatekeeper: Are you a heathen?

Alex: No.

Gatekeeper: Alex, what does Eid mean to you?

Alex: Nothing at all. I don't recall reading about it in the Quran.

Skylar: Alex why did you stop eating pork before giving up meat altogether?

Alex: I wanted to be respectful of Vasia and improve my health.

Icky: To be absolutely clear, it wasn't because you were personally leaning towards Islam?

Alex: No, pork is forbidden in Islam, but the Bible also says: 'The pig, though it has a split hoof completely divided, does not chew the cud; it is unclean for you. You must not eat their meat or touch their carcasses; they are unclean for you.'

Skylar: How do you feel about cows?

Alex: No particular feeling. Hindus consider the cow a sacred animal. When in shock, I have heard many people use the term 'holy cow'. The second chapter of the Quran is called 'The Cow' and if I remember correctly 'The Cow' is the Quran's longest chapter.

Skylar: It is the Quran's longest chapter.

Icky: In the Quran the chapter called 'The Cow' is before the chapter called 'The Woman'.

Skylar: There's no chapter in the Bible called 'The Woman'.

Icky: There's no chapter in the Bible called 'The Cow' either.

Ezra: Can we (speaking as to imitate a cow) moo-ve on. (pause) Gatekeeper, we are not getting anywhere.

Gatekeeper: No, we are not.

Ezra: Can you step it up?

Gatekeeper: Should women cover their hair?

Alex: Yes, if they want to and no, if they don't want to.

Skylar: I say yes and I always cover mine.

Icky: I say if you cover your hair, you're a stand pat.

Gatekeeper: What are your thoughts on Prophet Muhammad's marriages?

Skylar: Is that question necessary?

Icky: It's a good question.

Alex: I know where you are going with this. In the time and place I lived in many practises of both the Biblical and Quranic world would have been illegal. I understand Prophet Muhammad was an observer of the law of his time. I also understand Prophet Muhammad was an orphan and became a great man, I can relate to that.

Ezra: Gatekeeper, you could try a closed question.

Gatekeeper: Maybe I should. (pause) Alex, are homosexual relationships good or bad?

Alex: Both holy books are anti-homosexuality.

Gatekeeper: Are homosexual relationships good or bad?

Alex: If two homosexual people don't enjoy their relationship then it's a bad thing. Likewise, if two homosexual people enjoy their relationship then it's a good thing. Needless to say, the same rules apply in mixed-orientation relationships and heterosexual relationships.

Ezra: It's normally me who enjoys the view from the fence. Alex, your fence-sitting is remarkable.

Gatekeeper: Alex, is Jesus God?

Icky: Alex a simple yes will do.

Skylar: Or you can say he's a Prophet.

Alex: I don't believe Jesus ever called himself God or a Prophet, in either the Quran or the Bible.

Skylar: That's debatable!

Icky: It's not debatable!

Gatekeeper: What do you think of terrorism and who is to blame for it?

Alex: I blame the individual and their influences, whether it's a crusader or a jihadist.

Gatekeeper: Alex, help me break the deadlock here.

Alex: I don't have a specific view. I don't lean one way or the other; over the course of my life, I would say I dedicated an equal amount of time to both religions. (pause) Stole from the church and returned the money. (pause) Fell in love with a Muslim and broke her heart.

Gatekeeper: Who do you respect more, Malcolm X or Martin Luther King?

Skylar: Malcolm!

Icky: Martin!

Ezra: You two aren't going to agree on anything.

Gatekeeper: The question is for Alex.

Alex: I see them both as opposite sides of the same coin. To make progress both approaches operating at the same time were needed.

Skylar: Alex what do you think about the Ku Klux Klan calling themselves the 'Good Christian'?

Icky: Alex what do you think about Isis members shouting 'God is the greatest'?

Ezra: He thinks what I think, that religion is a waste of time and a system of control, which is actually totally out of control.

Alex: It has become that for many people. Most people follow the associated traditions of religion, but they do not follow the relevant holy book or live by its guidance.

Gatekeeper: Alex, you have been resolute. Skylar and Icky, I hope you have enjoyed your little clash.

Skylar: In accordance with my religion, I fight with those who fight with me.

Icky: I naturally turn the other cheek.

Gatekeeper: Unless anyone wants a consultation, we will now move on to talk about God.

Skylar: I would like a consultation with Christian. Sorry, I mean Icky.

Icky: I would be happy to re-educate you.

Narrator: Skylar and Icky enter the Consultation Zone.

Icky: Has one summoned me here for round two?

Skylar: No, I didn't.

Icky: Why are we here then?

Skylar: I don't think you're playing straight.

Icky: Explain.

Skylar: You said you want Alex put to Perpetual Sleep, but since your consultation with Ezra you seem to have promoted Hell.

Icky: Nonsense; utter nonsense!

Skylar: Did I misread the strange faces Ezra's been making?

Icky: I don't have a clue what you're talking about.

Skylar: Look, this is a man's afterlife you're playing with.

Icky: Aw, don't give me that hogwash! This is about you and I and us being ruled by that entitled narcissist Ezra.

Skylar: If Ezra's threatened or coerced you in any way you need to expose it. Remember, Malcolm X was the type of man who knew wrong was wrong, no matter how wrong was hidden.

Icky: Martin Luther King was the type of man who knew small disappointments were acceptable. Now let me tell you, this consultation is over.

Skylar: No, it's not!

Icky: Oh, really? Get lost!

Narrator: Icky walks out of the Consultation Zone and Skylar follows her back into position. Icky looks bemused and Skylar looks angry.

Gatekeeper: Is everything OK?

Skylar: Icky has something to say.

Icky: No, I don't!

Ezra: OK children, can we move on?

Gatekeeper: Yes, we will progress.

Alex: Good.

Gatekeeper: Alex, does God exist?

Alex: I don't know.

Ezra: Gatekeeper, how can you expect Alex to answer that?

Gatekeeper: By simply stating his opinion. Skylar and Icky, does God exist?

Skylar: Yes.

Icky: Yes.

Ezra: No way God exists.

Skylar: How do you think you're here now?

Icky: Who do you think makes the planets orbit the sun?

Alex: Interesting points.

Ezra: Why we're here and how the planets go around the sun are interesting, but it doesn't mean that God is behind it.

Gatekeeper: Who is behind it?

Ezra: I don't know.

Gatekeeper: Alex?

Alex: I'm not sure.

Ezra: Alex where was God when you were going through hard times?

Skylar: It was God who gave Alex access to the church's money so Alex could escape his adoptive father.

Alex: Why did God put me in that position in the first place?

Icky: It's the Devil that caused your plight; it's the Devil that makes bad things happen.

Ezra: God, the Devil. It was you Alex who stole and saved the church's money. Right or wrong it was you.

Alex: Hmm.

Ezra: If the Devil does exist, he is God's partner in crime, as nothing happens without God's permission. Right guys?

Skylar: God is great.

Ezra: Great doesn't mean good.

Icky: God is good.

Ezra: According to the good books, God is a mass murderer; he's easily jealous and hates hypocrites.

Skylar: Alex when you faced your most challenging moments you called on God.

Icky: Yeah, Alex why did you call on God during your most challenging moments? Deep down in the core of your being, you knew God would get you through.

Ezra: He was conditioned that way. Alex it was still you that stepped up and answered the challenge.

Gatekeeper: Alex, what do you have to say?

Alex: I don't know whether God exists, but I do acknowledge there is something out there more powerful than me and I also acknowledge that I'm not the author of my own existence.

Gatekeeper: I see. Thank you.

Skylar: Gatekeeper, I would like a consultation with Ezra.

Gatekeeper: OK, go on.

Narrator: Skylar and Ezra enter the Consultation Zone. Icky looks worried.

Chapter 7 –
What Could Have Been

Skylar: What's going on with you and Icky?

Ezra: I'm not sure what you mean.

Skylar: My consultation with Icky was quite alarming.

Ezra: Really?

Skylar: Yes, really. I would like to get your side of the story.

Ezra: I'm here like you are just trying to see us arrive at the best outcome for Alex.

Skylar: Why are you so crooked?

Ezra: Excuse me!

Skylar: For decades you've played Icky and me against each other.

Ezra: No, I have tolerated the two of you.

Skylar: Alex's afterlife is just a tiny component in your little game.

Ezra: Actually, Alex's afterlife is a massive component in my biggest game.

Skylar: You lack integrity and have poor ethics!

Ezra: You lack common sense and have dated morals!

Skylar: I will go out there and expose you.

Ezra: There's nothing to expose; you're clutching at straws. The state of play is I'm smarter than you and more important to this process than you and Icky combined.

Skylar: You really are just an entitled narcissist!

Ezra: That works for me.

Narrator: Skylar and Ezra return to their positions.

Gatekeeper: Alex, we are approaching the final stages of the discussion and I will shortly announce my determination. I would like to offer you the opportunity to ask five questions. Unfortunately, I cannot tell you about the first or last 1,000 days of your life. Your choice of questions will be considered in my decision-making process.

Alex: I don't really have anything I want to ask. Does anyone else have any suggestions?

Gatekeeper: Alex, similar to the super-ultra-interactive five-dimensional yellow-tide technology, which has allowed us all to be here, I have the ability to think at a level above and beyond what you are familiar with. I use 100% of my brain at all times.

Alex: I still don't have any questions. Maybe I will ask a question about the technology.

Ezra: Alex please don't waste this opportunity. I can ask the questions if you want.

Gatekeeper: Alex will ask the questions.

Alex: Erm (pause) OK. I have always wondered about what could have been. My first question is: what would my life have been like if at the age of 11 my adoptive father didn't stop me from playing football?

Gatekeeper: At an 89.5% chance you would have eventually played professional football. Your life would have been different; however, you would have still met Vasia at the mechanics and had a relationship with her.

Skylar: Wow!

Icky: Extraordinary.

Alex: Is that just a coincidence?

Gatekeeper: Is that your second question?

Ezra: It's a good question.

Alex: Gatekeeper, my second question is: in its basic form, what is coincidence?

Gatekeeper: Coincidence is when different forms of subconscious energy and other unseen components fuse with one another.

Icky: Vasia and Alex were drawn to each other.

Skylar: As if it was their destiny to meet.

Ezra: There's no such thing as destiny.

Alex: Interesting. (pause) Gatekeeper, my third question is: are our fates already determined, as in was everything that I had already done known before I did it?

Ezra: Basically, do we have freewill, or are all people just flowing along a pre-programmed path to the path's endpoint.

Alex: Exactly.

Gatekeeper: A person's endpoint, or events that take place throughout their life are not predetermined; however, there are patterns and subconscious routines that people follow, which is why people become predictable and are seen doing the same thing over and again in different ways.

Icky: I totally get it and I've always operated like that.

Skylar: I'm not sure I understand.

Gatekeeper: For example, I said there was an 89.5% chance that Alex would have been a professional footballer and still met Vasia. There was also a 10.5% chance that would not have happened. In one version of events, Alex coaches a football team and without ever meeting Jazzy gets married to Jazzy's business partner, Anisha. No versions of events are guaranteed until they are actually played out; however, it is safer to assume something predicted at a probability of 89.5% would come true.

Skylar: I now understand.

Gatekeeper: I knew you would. There was a near 100% chance you would.

Alex: Gatekeeper, my fourth question is: if I hadn't cheated on Vasia, what are all the possible things that could have happened?

Gatekeeper: That is a question I am sure you can answer yourself.

Alex: I would like to hear your answer though, please use bookmaker's odds.

Gatekeeper: Would you like it in ascending or descending order?

Alex: Most improbable first; descending order would be best.

Gatekeeper: At 10 to 1, Vasia would have ended the relationship with you, after you having an argument with her mother about Vasia buying you a heart-shaped man-bag.

Ezra: How on earth would a conversation like that have started? Wow, sorry, just thinking out loud.

Gatekeeper: At 6 to 1, Vasia, on one single occasion, would have had premarital sex with you and then left you for being a bad influence.

Icky: I could've seen that happening and if I was a gambler, I would have put money on it.

Gatekeeper: At 4 to 1, Vasia, would have had premarital sex with you and got pregnant.

Skylar: That would have been a big drama, especially in the Muslim community.

Gatekeeper: At near evens, Vasia would have asked you to convert to Islam.

Alex: You're right; I probably could have answered that question myself.

Gatekeeper: What is your fifth and final question?

Alex: I can't think of any more questions, I will ask you if anything comes to mind.

Gatekeeper: You can, but there may not be time. At this point I am ready to summarise and announce my determination.

Chapter 8 –
Do We Have An Agreement?

Alex: Ezra, before the determination I need a consultation with you.

Ezra: OK, let's go.

Narrator: Alex and Ezra enter the Consultation Zone.

Ezra: What do I owe the pleasure?

Alex: I need to find out about the past 1,000 days.

Ezra: Why? You still want to know how you died?

Alex: Yes, of course!

Ezra: I can't help you. Remember, I only know what you know. The Gatekeeper is the only person here who knows how you died and she's made it clear she is not going to tell you.

Alex: She may tell you though.

Ezra: If I obtain the information, what's in it for me?

Alex: What do you want?

Ezra: I want full control. After I tell you how you died, I want to make all your decisions for you.

Alex: Sounds like you want my soul. Are you the Devil or something?

Ezra: No, of course not. I'm definitely not.

Alex: Once you've told me how I died you want me to follow all of your instructions?

Ezra: Yes (pause) do we have an agreement?

Alex: Yes.

Ezra: OK, go back to the trial and tell the Gatekeeper I have requested a consultation.

Narrator: Alex leaves the Consultation Zone and signals the Gatekeeper to enter it. The Gatekeeper frowns before accepting. She enters the Consultation Zone, as Alex walks back to his position.

Gatekeeper: At this point, I am not sure there is anything you can say that is going to influence my determination.

Ezra: Gatekeeper, I want you to tell me how Alex died.

Gatekeeper: That is not something I am willing to do.

Ezra: I want to know!

Gatekeeper: I am happy to end this conversation here.

Ezra: My tolerance has gone and my civility is finished. Listen carefully, I have ruled Icky and Skylar for a long time, I know their strengths and weaknesses; I appreciate they are both significantly different, but figuratively they bleed through similar veins.

Gatekeeper: What are you saying?

Ezra: If you don't tell me what I want to know, I'll destroy Icky and Skylar. I'll do it, you'll have to carry that on your conscience and it will also damage Alex.

Gatekeeper: You really are a nasty piece of work.

Ezra: You're the one playing God. Now tell me what I want to know.

Gatekeeper: On one condition, you agree not to tell Alex.

Ezra: I agree. I won't tell Alex.

Gatekeeper: The Bishop stabbed Alex to death and secretly buried him in the cemetery.

Ezra: What? (pause) Why? (pause) Holy cow!

Gatekeeper: Alex recorded the Bishop admitting to being his real father and killing Alex's mother.

Ezra: The Bishop was Alex's real father? (pause) The Bishop killed Alex's mother and then killed Alex who was actually his son?

Gatekeeper: Yes.

Ezra: How did Alex know the Bishop was going to admit to being his real father and admit to killing Alex's mother?

Gatekeeper: Alex's adoptive father informed him that the Bishop pulled a few strings to arrange for Alex to be adopted by the Bishop's brother and he also informed him that 16 years later, the Bishop killed Alex's mother.

Ezra: Why on earth did the Bishop kill Alex's mother?

Gatekeeper: She was 15 at the time of Alex's birth and later threatened to expose the Bishop's conduct.

Ezra: What possessed Alex's adoptive father to tell him all of that?

Gatekeeper: Alex questioned his adoptive father about his childhood. He questioned his adoptive father whilst holding an unloaded military grade weapon. His adoptive father revealed the information out of fear.

Ezra: How did they come across each other in the first place?

Gatekeeper: After four years back in his hometown, Alex went to see his adoptive father; he at last had the courage to confront him about his childhood.

Ezra: Alex faced his demons, good for him.

Narrator: The Gatekeeper and Ezra return to their positions. Ezra beams a smug smile and dances on the spot.

Ezra: Alex, ready to know how you died?

Gatekeeper: You are not to tell Alex, you agreed you would not do that!

Ezra: I don't care what I agreed; that agreement's void.

Gatekeeper: Ezra, re-consider!

Ezra: Be quiet Gatekeeper! Alex this is how you died (pause) after four years back in your hometown you went to see your adoptive father. You took a weapon with you.

Icky: I see where this is going; Alex I knew you had it in you.

Ezra: It was an unloaded weapon.

Icky: Oh, stop it.

Ezra: You pointed the weapon at your adoptive father and proceeded to ask him questions. In a state of fear, he told you that the Bishop was your real father and your mother was 15 years old when she gave birth to you.

Skylar: The Bishop was Alex's real father. Now I see why the Bishop was so present.

Ezra: The Bishop pulled a few strings to ensure you were adopted by his brother.

Alex: How did I die?

Ezra: You went to see the Bishop and recorded him admitting to being your father.

Alex: I don't want to hear anymore; I guess he killed me so I couldn't expose the recording. If I exposed him, he would have gone to prison for sex with a minor and the impregnation of a minor.

Ezra: Yes, but there's more.

Alex: I don't want to hear anymore.

Ezra: I want you to hear it.

Alex: This is the problem with a rebellious ego.

Ezra: Yes, at times your father did have a rebellious ego.

Alex: I'm not talking about my father; I'm talking about you!

Ezra: What do you mean?

Alex: I'm on to you. I'm on to Icky and Skylar too.

Chapter 9 –
This Really Is The Death Of Me!

Ezra: Alex I instruct you not to say anything more.

Alex: You must be joking!

Ezra: We had a deal; you agreed!

Alex: (speaking as to sarcastically copy Ezra's voice) I don't care what I agreed; that agreement's void.

Icky: My agreement is void too.

Alex: What agreement?

Icky: I confess, Ezra pushed me into promoting an outcome of Hell instead of Perpetual Sleep.

Skylar: I knew it!

Gatekeeper: The initial deception was quite obvious; however, it actually helped the process. Another thing that was obvious was Alex using one of his proverbial animal traps to capture the information about his death. Alex, as a goodwill gesture can you let me know if I have the right idea?

Alex: OK.

Gatekeeper: In consultation with Ezra, you agreed that you would give him some seeds. In that instance Ezra was the red squirrel and the seeds were the authority to make all of your decisions. Ezra due to his nature, without even realising it, became trapped and was bait for me, in that instance I was the fox. Ezra again, without even realising it, trapped me with a threat to destroy Icky and Skylar.

Alex: Right so far.

Skylar: Ezra you disgust me!

Icky: Ezra you're lower than the flies that feast on the fresh excrement of a sick pig! (pause) Maybe confession is good for the soul after all.

Alex: Gatekeeper, continue.

Gatekeeper: You said that once you have both the squirrel and fox trapped you stop feeding the squirrel, let it die, gut it and sell it. You said the fox would stay alive for a more elaborate game, which I assume is this process.

Alex: You really do use 100% of your brain.

Ezra: What about me? Nobody is thinking about how this affects me!

Skylar: Ezra you're dead to me!

Icky: Ezra you've been well and truly gutted.

Gatekeeper: Now you can get stuffed. Ezra, please leave the process.

Ezra: This really is the death of me!

Narrator: Ezra exits the Temple on Alex's left-hand side.

Alex: I just killed my Ego. (pause) Now, Skylar and Icky, as I said I'm on to you.

Gatekeeper: Maybe so.

Alex: Ezra was my Ego in human form.

Gatekeeper: Correct.

Alex: I think the super-ultra-interactive five-dimensional yellow-tide technology enabled my thoughts to become human beings.

Gatekeeper: Yes, it ensures the fairest trial possible.

Alex: Skylar is my Super-Ego and Icky is my Id.

Gatekeeper: How and when did you figure this out?

Alex: Early on in the process I asked you: 'why can't I hear all of my thoughts?' You said they would shortly reach me. I have only been reached by Skylar, Icky and Ezra.

Skylar: At that point, had you already worked it out?

Alex: No, I just thought it was strange, but this whole process is strange. Thinking back, your full names spell out who you are; Skylar Erakat and Super Ego share the same initials, Ezra Goodwin-O'Fallon's initials spell Ego and Id and Icky Downing also matches.

Icky: How and when did you unearth our true identities?

Alex: Under pressure I think quickly and there were moments when all three of you individually spoke as quickly and as repetitively as I usually think. I also figured someone as peculiar as Ezra must have been created by technology; however, I was only certain when Ezra didn't want me asking questions about the technology. Naturally, if Ezra was created by technology then so were both of you. I then asked myself, what are the three of you modelled on and what gives you the right to be in my trial?

Gatekeeper: Yes, I understand that and a verbal examination of the technology would have unmasked the trio.

Alex: Really?

Gatekeeper: Yes. Icky and Skylar are there any parting questions or comments you would like to make?

Icky: I have some questions.

Skylar: I have a comment to make.

Gatekeeper: Icky, please ask your questions.

Icky: Firstly, can you dissect the super-ultra-interactive five-dimensional yellow-tide technology? Secondly, can you explain why you can use 100% of your brain? Lastly, why can't the ordinary mortal remember their first or last 1,000 days on earth?

Gatekeeper: OK. (pause) *Super* represents the instantaneous action of commands; *ultra* represents the separation and analysis of components; *interactive* represents the interactions of different components; the first three dimensions are physical: height, width and depth, the fourth dimension is spiritual and the *fifth dimension* is telekinetic; Infrared covers five meters, Bluetooth covers ten meters and *Yellow-Tide* is limitless; *technology* is the internal mechanics, which allow for the translocation of all the featured elements.

Icky: Magnificent.

Gatekeeper: Super-ultra-interactive five-dimensional yellow-tide technology, is used on all gatekeepers to allow them to use 100% of their brain. Using 100% of my brain is necessary for my judgement and remembering events that others cannot. The ordinary mortal has not evolved to the level of being able to remember like a Gatekeeper. (pause) Skylar, please make your comment.

Skylar: Alex there have been numerous occasions where Ezra has made composite decisions for you. In fact, Ezra often makes decisions for all of us. It could be better to side with one of us rather than accept Ezra's mediation.

Alex: Please help me understand what you're saying.

Skylar: I think I can. I was the voice in your head that said: 'marry Vasia and convert to Islam.' I then went on to say: 'you wouldn't be converting; you would actually just start living in accordance with your true nature.'

Icky: I said: 'leave Vasia and have some fun, sleep around for a bit.'

Skylar: Ezra mediated and forced his opinion on to you, so you then slept with a sex worker thinking you could stay in a relationship with Vasia.

Icky: Acting on either my or Skylar's presentation would have been best for you.

Alex: I understand. Has there ever been a time when I agreed with one of you?

Skylar: Yes, I was the voice in your head that said not to buy bullets for the military grade weapons. Icky advised you to purchase enough bullets to kill an army and Ezra demanded that at least one of the weapons be fully loaded. I was pleased you sided with me.

Icky: You listened to me when I said: 'steal £20 a week from the church.' Skylar didn't particularly want you to steal anything and Ezra wanted you to steal a large amount of cash on one solitary occasion.

Alex: I totally get it. Are there any occasions where I didn't listen to all three of you?

Skylar: You make decisions ignoring our influences quite often. The most significant example of you ignoring the three of us is when you would communicate with the Bishop, we always had reservations about him and were all against his influence.

Gatekeeper: The Bishop being your biological father meant there were unseen links and magnetism between the two of you. The Bishop was your primary external influence.

Alex: That's all enlightening. I don't think I ever did anything that I wasn't supposed to do.

Gatekeeper: No, you didn't do anything you didn't think you could get away with.

Alex: Same difference.

Gatekeeper: Two wrongs do not make a right and double negatives do not always make a positive.

Alex: Yes, I acknowledge and understand that a double negative disposition is not the same as having a positive outlook.

Gatekeeper: It does not take much wisdom to acknowledge and understand that. (pause) Icky and Skylar you may leave the process, thank you for your contribution.

Icky: Alex it's been an anomalous experience.

Skylar: All the best Alex.

Narrator: Icky and Skylar exit the Temple on Alex's left-hand side.

Gatekeeper: Alex, all of your thoughts will shortly return to your mind. Icky, Skylar and Ezra will exist only in your mind and you will revert back to hearing them in your own voice as is typical.

Alex: I understand. Gatekeeper, I haven't figured out your role in all of this.

Chapter 10 –
Irreversible Determination

Gatekeeper: I am the Gatekeeper and it is time for me to announce my determination; my determination will confirm your outcome.

Alex: Earlier, you allowed me to ask you five questions and I didn't ask my last question; I would like to ask it now.

Gatekeeper: You can ask it after I announce this determination. Do not speak until I instruct you to do so.

Alex: OK, but in my silence and the acceptance of my death, please take into consideration that I died in my 30s, just like Martin Luther King, Malcolm X and Jesus. (pause) The good die young.

Gatekeeper: After living 1,001 days or more, when someone has died, he or she faces judgement. If that person's good deeds exceed their bad deeds, they go to Heaven. If that person's bad deeds exceed their good deeds, they go to Hell. In special circumstances, such as a Gatekeeper being undecided at the end of a trial, a person may go back to Earth via Reincarnation. In highly unusual circumstances, such as a person desiring to go to Hell without justification, a person may be put to Perpetual Sleep. Alexander, we have concluded your afterlife trial discussion and several afterlife consultations have taken place. I deem the circumstances that brought you to this moment, unique, although not special or unusual. (pause) In summary, you have lived a life of great duality and in today's process you have also demonstrated a double-sided nature, though not a nature of double standards. In your life the bad deeds of others handicapped you and despite a few indiscretions you worked to make things better. In the right environment I believe you will be a force for good, nevertheless your bad deeds must not go unpunished. (pause) With an ambivalent mind I determine that you will be placed in Hell (pause) for a period of 13 days (pause) before being permanently placed in Heaven. That is my irreversible determination. For a short time, you will be **Hell's Good Guy**. (pause) Alex, you wanted to ask me a final question. I will answer the question and then you will stay here and await transportation to Hell. You are now free to speak.

Alex: Gatekeeper, with some of the facts established today, I now have cogitation for my mother. My last question is: after giving birth to me and giving me up, what happened to her?

Gatekeeper: In a nutshell, the pregnancy made her an outcast in the community. After delivering you in the early part of June, your mother travelled to a new community; however, just a week and six days after you had left for the new city to start your new life, your mother returned home looking for you. (pause) She threatened to expose the Bishop if she was not put in contact with you. The Bishop killed her on the same day (pause) your mother died at the age of 31 and she was secretly buried in the cemetery under plot 13, exactly like you were 18 years later.

Alex: Oh my (pause) unlucky number 13, it's such a punishing number. (pause) This is all completely soul-destroying.

Gatekeeper: Alex, your mother was murdered; she went to Heaven and became a Gatekeeper. Finally, your mother has just conducted an afterlife trial without engaging in nepotism. (pause) I'll see you again, son!

Narrator: Alex's mother, the Gatekeeper, exits the Temple on Alex's left-hand side. The Temple lights start to fade.

A Story For Another Day –
Perspective A

Narrator: Experience **Jazzy**, Anisha and Sam's early morning meeting from **Jazzy's perspective**.

Jazzy: Thanks for coming guys.

Anisha: An 8:00 a.m. meeting, this better be important. You interrupted me studying for my acting degree.

Sam: This is an early one Jazz. (speaking with laughter) Are you trying to make up for the clocks going forward last week?

Jazzy: No. I've called you to the restaurant to show you this fantastic poster.

Anisha: It's a smaller than usual plate of fish, chips, peas and tartar sauce.

Jazzy: I want to run a promotion selling a cheaper plate of fish and chips.

Anisha: OK.

Jazzy: The plan is to have people coming through the door nonstop.

Anisha: What price do you want to sell it at?

Jazzy: As cheap as possible; 3 pence below cost, £4s.

Anisha: It will get people in the restaurant, but it makes no sense selling anything below a 90% mark up. Just under £8 should be the selling price.

Jazzy: No. (pause) As equal partners, when we can't agree we should compromise.

Anisha: Well, we can either let our head of operations decide or meet in the middle.

Sam: I can tell you both right now that selling at a loss, or even selling at £8 a plate makes no sense. We would be giving the food away and my chefs would be swamped in the kitchen.

Jazzy: If we don't sell at £4s, we won't sell all of the fish I've ordered.

Anisha: How much did you order?

Jazzy: Well (pause) I meant to order 100 kilos of fish but I inadvertently ordered 100 boxes.

Sam: That's 1,000 kilos!

Anisha: That's 100 boxes!

Jazzy: (speaking carefree) I already said it's 100 boxes.

Anisha: (speaking with anger) You're such a tart Jazz.

Jazzy: A tart? This is about the fish, right?

Sam: I'm going for a walk (speaking with slight disappointment) see if I can think up a solution.

Narrator: Sam exits the room.

Anisha: I've worked too hard to have you constantly ruining everything. We're almost at the end of the tax year and I'm not going to have you constantly wiping out profits.

Jazzy: We all make mistakes, besides it's a drop in the ocean.

Anisha: You make more mistakes than the weatherman. One of these days you're going to give me a heart attack.

Jazzy: (speaking carefree) You need to lighten up, be like a *wave* in the sea and *skate* over things.

Anisha: I don't appreciate you making fish jokes. (speaking with force) I'm selling my share of the business.

Jazzy: (speaking carefree) Be sure to charge *cod*. Cash on demand.

Anisha: Stop being silly. Did you buy the fish from our usual supplier? Have you tried to return it?

Jazzy: Yes, I tried and I spoke to *Amber Jack* and *Mr Sturgeon* yesterday, but they said it's our problem.

Anisha: Amber Jack and Sturgeon are names of fish.

Jazzy: Yes, I know. They obviously use those names as gimmicks, but the phone call was genuine.

Anisha: (speaking with a raised voice) Why are you doing this? We're meant to be family.

Jazzy: We're third cousins, hardly family.

Anisha: Is this because I got involved with Mani Anderson from the wholesalers? I told you that I called everything off once I realised you had already been there.

Jazzy: I had one costly date with him. Mani didn't bring his wallet and didn't pay me back.

Anisha: (speaking with malice) And you still spent the night with him.

Jazzy: We had one date ages ago. Mani's got nothing to do with the price of fish and I don't like the term: (speaking slowly) 'already been there.'

Anisha: You had one night with him and then he gave you the cold shoulder (pause) harsh.

Jazzy: We both agreed Mani is a criminal and takes advantage both personally and professionally. We also agreed not to buy from him or communicate with him and that's all there is to it.

Anisha: I admitted I went there with Mani; you won't admit that you went there too and wanted more. He used you; he wanted me for one night and possibly more. I actually called it off, but ever since then you've been jealous, ruining the business to punish me. Am I wrong?

Jazzy: You're just fishing for information now.

Anisha: Alright, let's work out what we're going to do about this oversupply of fish.

Jazzy: No need. (pause) Happy April Fools. (pause) I was joking about the fish and I'll admit I did go there with Mani.

Anisha: (speaking with pain) My chest (pause) my chest, it's like a sledge-hammer hitting my chest. (pause) (speaking whilst holding breath) I can't breathe.

Narrator: Jazz quickly dials 9-9-9.

Jazzy: (long pause) (speaking with concern) I need an ambulance please. OK. (pause) Yes, I need an ambulance, my cousin is having some sort of shock or heart attack. (pause) Well, she's out of breath laying on her side on the floor. She's flopping around like a fish fighting for air. (speaking with awareness) Oh, erm, I'm sorry I think I may have wasted your time. I think she's pranking me.

Anisha: (laughter) (laughter stops) Two can play that game. Happy April Fools right back at you.

Jazzy: OK get up. Putting that acting degree to full use I see.

Anisha: Yes. (laughter) (laughter stops) Oh and I knew Mani battered your fish, if you know what I mean.

Narrator: Sam re-enters the room.

Sam: Ladies, I'm back, everything is sorted. (pause) I've been on the phone with Mani from Mani's wholesalers. Our bank account's now empty, but I've bought enough mix to batter 1,000 kilos of fish. Mani was happy to help, he said he will personally deliver the goods later today and even have a battered fish.

Anisha: (speaking with anger) Sam.

Jazzy: (speaking with a raised voice) Shit.

A Story For Another Day –
Perspective B

Narrator: Experience Jazzy, **Anisha** and Sam's early morning meeting from **Anisha's perspective**.

Jazzy: Thanks for coming guys.

Anisha: This better be good. You interrupted me studying for my acting degree.

Sam: This is an early one Jazz. (speaking with annoyance) Are you trying to make up for the clocks going forward last week?

Jazzy: No. I've called you to the restaurant to show you this poster.

Anisha: It's a smaller than usual plate of fish and chips, with peas and tartar sauce.

Jazzy: I want to run a promotion selling a cheaper plate of fish and chips.

Anisha: Why? What's the plan?

Jazzy: The plan is to have people constantly coming through the door.

Anisha: What price do you want to sell it at?

Jazzy: As low as possible; a few pence below cost, £4.

Anisha: (speaking with force) Huh, £4. It will get people in the restaurant, but it makes no sense selling anything below a 90% mark up. Just under £8 should be the selling price.

Jazzy: No. I'm not having that.

Anisha: Well, if we can't agree we should meet in the middle or let Sam decide.

Sam: Anisha's right; this makes no sense. We would be giving the food away and my chefs would be swamped.

Jazzy: If we don't sell at £4, we won't sell all the fish I've got in.

Sam: Exactly how much did you order?

Jazzy: Well (pause) I meant to order 100 kilos of fish but I accidentally ordered 100 boxes.

Anisha: That's 1,000 kilos! I should kick your arse.

Sam: That's 100 boxes!

Jazzy: (speaking carefree) I already said it's 100 boxes.

Anisha: (speaking with anger) Jazzy you're such an airheaded tart.

Jazzy: Oh really? This is still about the fish?

Sam: I'm going for a walk (speaking with slight disappointment) I'll see if I can sort this.

Narrator: Sam exits the room.

Anisha: I've worked too hard to have you constantly ruining everything. We're almost at the end of the tax year and I'm not going to have you constantly wiping out my profits.

Jazzy: (speaking carefree) We all make mistakes.

Anisha: One of these weeks you're gonna give me a heart attack.

Jazzy: (speaking carefree) You need to lighten up, be like a *wave* in the sea and *skate* over things.

Anisha: I don't appreciate you making fish jokes. (speaking with force) I'm going to think seriously about selling my shares in the business.

Jazzy: (speaking carefree) Be sure to ask for *cod*. Cash on demand.

Anisha: (speaking with anger) Stop being stupid. Did you buy the fish from Fresh Fish Supplies or W. Seaman? Can you return it?

Jazzy: No, I tried. I spoke to *Amber Jack* and *Michael Sturgeon* yesterday, they said it's your problem.

Anisha: Something about this whole thing stinks.

Jazzy: I know it seems *fishy* but we all make mistakes.

Anisha: (speaking with confusion) Why are you doing this? We're meant to be family.

Jazzy: Family? We're distant cousins at best.

Anisha: Is this because I got involved with Mani Anderson from the wholesalers? I told you that I called everything off once I found out you had already been there.

Jazzy: I had one costly date with him. Mani didn't bring his wallet and didn't pay me back.

Anisha: And you still spent the night with him.

Jazzy: We had one date. Mani's got nothing to do with this situation and I don't like the term: 'already been there.'

Anisha: You had one night with him and then got the cold shoulder.

Jazzy: We agreed Mani is a user and personally and professionally takes advantage. We also agreed not to buy from him or communicate with him and that's all there is to it.

Anisha: I admitted I went there with Mani; you won't admit that you went there too and wanted more. He used you; he wanted me for one night and possibly more. I actually called it off, but ever since then you've been jealous, ruining the business to punish me. Confess it all!

Jazzy: You're turning this into a fishing expedition.

Anisha: Yeah, whatever. Let's work out what we're going to do about all this extra fish.

Jazzy: No need. (pause) Happy April Fools. (pause) I was joking about the fish and I'll admit I did go there with Mani. Mani was a lot of fun even if it was for one night.

Anisha: (speaking with pain) My chest (pause) my chest, it's like a hammer is hitting my chest. (pause) (speaking whilst exhaling) I can't breathe.

Narrator: Jazz quickly dials 9-9-9.

Jazzy: (long pause) (speaking with concern) I need an ambulance now. (pause) (speaking with serious concern) OK, I'm calm. (pause) Yes, I need an ambulance, my cousin is having a heart attack. She's flopping around like a fish fighting for air. (speaking with awareness) Oh, erm, I'm sorry, I think I may have wasted your time. I think she's playing a practical joke on me.

Anisha: (laughter) (laughter stops) Two can play that game. Happy April Fools to you too.

Jazzy: OK get up. (pause) You'll definitely qualify as an actor.

Anisha: Yeah, I will. (laughter) (laughter stops) Oh and I knew Mani battered your fish, if you know what I mean.

Narrator: Sam re-enters the room.

Sam: Ladies, I'm back, everything is sorted. (pause) I've been on the phone with Mani. It's cost a bomb, but I've bought enough batter for tons of fish. Mani was happy to help. He gave me a big discount on the condition we don't return any batter.

Anisha: (speaking with anger) Damn it Sam.

Jazzy: (speaking with a raised voice) Oh shit.

A Story For Another Day –
Perspective C

Narrator: Experience Jazzy, Anisha and **Sam's** early morning meeting from **Sam's perspective**.

Sam: Morning ladies.

Jazzy: Thanks for coming Sam.

Anisha: This better be good. You interrupted me studying for my acting degree.

Sam: This is an early one Jazz. (speaking with annoyance) Are you trying to make up for the clocks going forward?

Jazzy: No. I've called you out your gaff to show you this poster.

Anisha: It's a smaller than usual plate of fish and chips, with peas and tartar sauce.

Jazzy: I want to run a promo selling a cheaper plate of fish and chips. (pause) The plan is to have people coming through the door nonstop. We can sell it at £4.

Anisha: It will get people in the restaurant, but it makes no sense selling anything below a 99% mark up. I say £8 should be the selling price.

Jazzy: No. (pause) As equal partners, where we can't agree we should compromise.

Anisha: Well, we can either let our head chef decide or meet in the middle.

Sam: I can tell you both right now that selling that plate at a loss, or even selling it at £8 a plate makes no sense. We would be giving the food away and my chefs would be swamped in the kitchen.

Jazzy: If we don't sell at £4, we won't sell all the fish I've had delivered.

Anisha: How much did you order?

Jazzy: Well (pause) I meant to order 100 kilos of fish but I accidentally ordered 100 boxes.

Sam: That's 1,000 kilos.

Jazzy: (speaking casually) 100 boxes.

Anisha: (speaking with anger) You're such a tart Jazz.

Jazzy: (speaking carefree) A tart? This is about the fish, isn't it?

Sam: I'm going for a walk (speaking with insincere disappointment) see if I can think up a solution.

Narrator: Sam exits the room and listens in from the kitchen.

Anisha: I have worked too hard to have you constantly ruining everything. We are almost at the end of the tax year and I'm not going to have you constantly wiping out our profits.

Jazzy: (speaking carefree) You need to lighten up, be like a *wave* in the sea and *skate* past things.

Anisha: I do not appreciate you making fish jokes. (speaking seriously) I am going to seriously think about selling my shares in the business.

Jazzy: (speaking carefree) Be sure to get *cod* for your shares. *Cash on demand.*

Anisha: (speaking with anger) Stop being stupid. Did you buy the fish from Fresh Fish Supplies or W. Seamans? Can you return it?

Jazzy: No, I tried. I spoke to *Amber Jack* and *Michael Sturgeon* from Fresh Fish Supplies, they said it's our problem.

Anisha: Amber Jack and Sturgeon are names of fish.

Jazzy: Yes, I know. They obviously use those names as gimmicks, but the phone call was genuine.

Anisha: Something about this whole thing stinks.

Jazzy: I know it seems *fishy* but we all make mistakes.

Anisha: (speaking with anger) Why are you doing this? We are meant to be family.

Jazzy: We're distant cousins.

Narrator: Sam makes a phone call in the kitchen.

Sam: Mani, it's Fouler. Guess what?

Mani: What?

Sam: I'm eavesdropping on your girlfriends arguing about the latest shenanigans.

Mani: What's happened?

Sam: I think Jazz might be playing an April Fool's joke on Anisha, but whether she is or isn't we can benefit.

Mani: How so?

Sam: I need enough fish batter mix to batter 1,000 kilos of fish, in fact double that.

Mani: I can get you enough for half of that. I'll provide you with enough ingredients to make up the rest.

Sam: What's the cheapest you can do it for?

Mani: Around 5 g's (speaking quickly) I mean 6 g's (pause) (speaking with excitement) yeah 6 g's. I can do it for you for £6,000.

Sam: I'm transferring you 7 g's from the company account as we speak. Bring the goods round this afternoon and bring me a grand in cash. I'll cook you up a nice battered fish.

Mani: What if Anisha or Jazzy want to return it, or they work out that you've bought in bulk without a discount?

Sam: Those two are clueless and know sod all. Remember it was me who told you to one-night stand Jazz and then move on to Anisha. It was me who told Anisha you slept with Jazz to distract her from me dipping into the takings. (speaking with confidence) Don't worry about anything, I've got this.

Mani: OK cool. I've got to drop off some rifles for Alex, then visit Lenny Jackson; I'll get on to this around eleven-ish.

Sam: I'll go and let the skirts know that we've got batter coming. Speak later. (long pause).

Narrator: Sam exits the kitchen.

Sam: Ladies, I'm back, everything's sorted. (pause) I've been on the phone with Mani. It's cost a bomb, but I've bought enough batter to batter tons of fish. Mani was happy to help. He gave me a massive discount on the condition we don't return any batter.

Anisha: (speaking with anger) Damn it Sam. It was just an April Fool's joke.

Jazzy: (speaking with a raised voice) Shit.

Sam: (speaking softly) I'm so sorry, I didn't realise. We better order 100 boxes of fish on the company credit card and run with the £4 promotion.

Jazzy: (speaking with a raised voice) Oh shit.

Afterword – By Samantha Carbon

Hell's Good Guy is a refreshing reminder of how much the unconscious mind informs our thinking, feelings and behaviours. It's a journey involving the uncertainty of destination but a certainty of upheaval and disturbances. The main character positions himself in space and in time which mirrors how he spatially situated himself with all who made contact with him.

Alex's opportunity to have a frank and often explicit conversation with his ego, super-ego & id allows the reader to fantasise about what may be buried within their own deep structures. Moreover, the reader is reminded that we are always engaged in acts of self-management from the choices of vocation, perception and the facilitation of our needs.

Over Alex's lifetime, we get a sense of how much the mind objectifies, knows and relates to different ways of being, and how his choices have informed different outcomes. His reflection and understanding of his experiences in life have not only conjured repressed wishes, but they have also stimulated ego, super-ego & id memories. On the other hand, his choices in life can be viewed as unconscious attempts to gain control over painful situations hoping they can one day lead to mastery and resolution.

Alex's dialogue with his ego, super-ego & id raises the awareness of faults, strengths and imperfections, along with unmet needs masked or never expressed. The conversation changes the illusion of his reality by challenging what has happened to him to falsifying what may happen to him in the present.

The risks taken and the uncertainties experienced have been inescapable existential challenges. Alex's subvocal engagement is an ordinary feature that many shy away from and by confronting his unconscious theatre; we temporarily enjoy the illusion of managing the ego, super-ego & id and recognise life as a bewildering drama. This has given the reader a sense of novelty and understanding of how much our internal dialogue motivates and encourages us to survive.

Samantha Carbon – Psychotherapist and Clinical Supervisor

###

9 781527 283138